YOU ARE THE LIGHT OF THE WORLD

YOU ARE THE LIGHT OF THE WORLD

Sermons on the New Testament

⇊

Jack R. Lundbom

WIPF & STOCK · Eugene, Oregon

YOU ARE THE LIGHT OF THE WORLD
Sermons on the New Testament

Copyright © 2024 Jack R. Lundbom. All rights reserved. Except for brief quotations in critical publications or reviews, no part of this book may be reproduced in any manner without prior written permission from the publisher. Write: Permissions, Wipf and Stock Publishers, 199 W. 8th Ave., Suite 3, Eugene, OR 97401.

Wipf & Stock
An Imprint of Wipf and Stock Publishers
199 W. 8th Ave., Suite 3
Eugene, OR 97401

www.wipfandstock.com

PAPERBACK ISBN: 979-8-3852-2660-3
HARDCOVER ISBN: 979-8-3852-2661-0
EBOOK ISBN: 979-8-3852-2662-7

Contents

Abbreviations vii
Preface ix

Advent
    1 The Coming Battle 3
    2 The Coming Kingship 7
    3 The Coming Order 10
    4 The Coming God 16
    5 The Coming Banquet 21

Christmas
    6 Room for Jesus 27

Prayer Week
    7 "Our Father in Heaven, Hallowed Be Your Name" 35
    8 "Your Kingdom Come, Your Will Be Done" 41
    9 "Give Us This Day Our Daily Bread" 47
  10 "Forgive Us Our Debts" 52
  11 "Deliver Us From Evil" 57

Lent
  12 "The Whole of Creation Waits" 65

Holy Week
  13 "It Is Expedient that One Man Should Die" 73

Contents

- 14 "Father Forgive Them, for They Know Not What They Do" 79
- 15 "Today You Will Be with Me in Paradise" 82
- 16 "Woman, Here Is Your Son . . . Here Is Your Mother" 85
- 17 "My God, My God, Why Have You Forsaken Me?" 89
- 18 "I Am Thrsty" 92
- 19 "It Is Finished" 95
- 20 "Father, Into Your Hands I Commend My Spirit" 98

Easter
- 21 "If Christ Be Not Risen . . ." 103
- 22 "Work Out Your Own Faith with Fear and Trembling" 109

Season of Pentecost
- 23 "When I Was a Child" 117
- 24 Pilgrims Here, Settlers There 122
- 25 "You Are the Salt of the Earth" 128
- 26 "You Are the Light of the World" 134
- 27 Authority from Above or Below? 140
- 28 Lessons from Greek Games 145
- 29 Abraham Obeyed 150
- 30 And Sarah Laughed 155

All Saints
- 31 "A Bride Adorned for Her Husband" 163
- 32 Is It Well With Your Soul? 168

Name Index 173
Scripture Index 175

Abbreviations

JB	The Jerusalem Bible
KJV	The King James Version
LXX	The Septuagint
MSS	Manuscripts
NAB	New American Bible
NEB	New English Bible
NIV	New International Version
NRSV	The New Revised Standard Version
NT	New Testament
OT	Old Testament
REB	Revised English Bible
RSV	The Revised Standard Version

Preface

THE PRESENT COLLECTION OF sermons, all on texts of the New Testament, were preached in churches I served as pastor or in joint services between our church and another in town. Unlike previously published collections, they follow more or less the church year: a series on the coming events in Salvation History for Advent; a Christmas sermon; a series on the Lord's Prayer for Prayer Week beginning the New Year; a Lenten sermon; Jesus' Seven Last Words from the cross for Holy Week; two Easter sermons; a collection of sermons for the season of Pentecost, two of which are on Jesus' words in Matt 5:13-16 of his "Sermon on the Mount;" and two concluding sermons for All Saints Sunday.

Scriptural quotations are largely from the *New Revised Standard Verson*, although some are from the *Revised Standard Version and other modern English Versions.*

Jack R. Lundbom

Advent

1

The Coming Battle[1]

Text: Luke 16:16

The law and the prophets were until John; since then the good news of the kingdom of God is preached, and every one enters it violently

THE WORKING OUT OF God's plan of salvation has its model in a sequence of events that was familiar to peoples of antiquity. We have seen the plan in the coming of Jesus to earth: what led up to his coming, what happened while he ministered on earth, and what resulted from his victory on the cross. Something similar is promised at the end of time—a reenactment of the earlier plan but with significant reversals and a different outcome.

Because the coming of Jesus centuries ago and his coming again are God's two great dramas acted out on the historical stage, parallel and informing one another, we keep them together during Advent. We celebrate Jesus' first coming, and we anticipate his coming again. The church relives the past; it lives in the present;

---

1. Preached in the Covenant Church of Thomaston, CT, on December 2, 1984.

it anticipates a future already begun. The Christian life transcends historical time.

God's plan of salvation is modeled on the exchange of power seen to take place between nations. We have seen it in modern times when Napoleon of France was defeated, when Hitler of Germany was toppled, when the Emperor of Japan was dethroned. It has happened many other times. People in antiquity saw empires come and go. The great Assyrian empire crumbled in the seventh century B.C. It came about gradually. In 655 Egypt declared its independence and in 652 civil war erupted in Assyria. Then after a few years of stability, King Assurbanipal of Assyria died and a revolt followed; in 626 Nabopolassar proclaimed himself king of Babylon in the southern part of the empire; and in 612 Nineveh fell; Assyria was no more. Nebuchadnezzar of Babylon was now king of the world. The Babylonian empire restored order and went on to build great buildings. The change was culminated with celebrations for the victor.

In Revelation, the most difficult biblical book to understand, the End Times is depicted in simiar terms. I will give only a broad sweep. Seven churches of Asia Minor (presently Western Turkey) are given a message from God to "clean up their act" before the drama begins. Each has its problems, and the Lord sends messengers to warn them and tell them what to do.

We learn then about activity going on in heaven. The scroll with God's hidden agenda is sealed and only the Lamb, who is Jesus, can open it. When it is opened, we discover that peace is to be taken from the earth (Rev 6:4), which is to say strife will now begin and gradually grow in intensity until the climactic battle occurs between the Lamb and kings of this world (Revelation 17). The "tribulation," as it is called, comes on gradually. The reason is probably that God is slow to anger. During this time of testing God's people are shown to be what they are. Galliant martyrs for the faith go first and await final victory. Then the 144,000 (a symbolic figure) are gathered from earth to the singing of the great multitude in heaven; these have already washed their robes in the blood of the Lamb (Revelation 7). Others are saved gradually as times get increasingly difficult and the forces of evil become stronger (Revelation 13).

Then those still on earth are brought to give glory to God when they hear the choir of 144,000 sing from an upper chamber, telling them to "fear God and give him glory" (Rev 14:6–7). Those who remain steadfast, keep the commandments of God, and have faith in Jesus will be blessed when they die (Rev 14:12–13). Then comes the harvest about which Matthew speaks: tares are separated from the wheat. These are those who could not be rooted out earlier lest others be destroyed (Matt 13:24–30).

In Revelation 15 all who have been won for the kingdom are singing the song of Moses and the song of the Lamb, i.e., some old songs and some new. Wrath for those saved is now ended. Revelation 16 describes the final act of God's wrath. If it came on slowly, it will end in a fury. Hardened souls on earth are heard cursing God and refusing to give him the glory. As a result he descends on them like he descended on Egypt with the plagues. The intense wrath of God is more than a match for the intense turpitude of humanity.

The final battle takes place on Mount Megiddo (Hebrew *harmageddon*), which need not concern us because hopefully we are not there for this latter day "Masada." The term appears to be cryptic, for while Megiddo is built on rock, it is not really a mountain. In Revelation 17 Jesus defeats the harlot of Babylon, another cryptic term for the final powers on earth. Jesus is then proclaimed King of kings and Lord of lords. What follows is the new order; the new creation; the wedding of Christ and the church; and a final banquet of celebration.

This is only a vision, so we must be careful not to take all its details literally and interpret them as a clear picture of the End Times, which it is not. Presented in Revelation is a story-like preview of what is to come, but something that will surely take place. Having given this caution, we must be just as careful not to write off John's dream as if it is nothing at all. We may do that with our own dreams, but not with this one. There will be an end of time; there will be a warning to churches to get ready; there will be a build-up of evil and a build-up of God's wrath, also a gradual refining of the faithful to see whether they are real gold or plated imitation; there will be a final burst of God's wrath upon the wicked and Jesus will emerge as King of kings, Lord of lords; and there will be a new creation and a great celebration to culminate it all, which we call Heaven and the Heavenly Banquet.

The coming battle is not to frighten us, for by the time it takes place all those among the saved are in the heavenly choir or being fitted for robes. For them the tribulation is past and battles fought are now behind them. This brings me to my text, which says that those who enter the kingdom do so violently. How violently it is not said. Some more violently than others; some less; some gradually. What Jesus is trying to tell people is that becoming his follower and being reconciled to God is a battle of sorts that we all have to fight and win. This saves us from the terrible battle at the end for those who continue to be stubbornly rebellious.

Today we meet with some of our young people about to join the church. Others will come when they are ready. I have seen a bit of a battle in almost every one of them, but am sure I do not know the whole of it. I expect that even after they have become church members they will have times when they do battle with God and his Christ. Some may enter the kingdom violently; others may have smaller eruptions. This has to occur. But in the end is the peace the gospel promises.

These young people need to know that each of us has a story to tell about how we struggled with God to enter his kingdom, which is God's rule over our lives. They are not alone. And if others of you are still engaged in some sort of battle, you also are not alone. Let us pray for each and every person we know of today who finds that entering the kingdom of God is a battle, a battle that must be fought and won for his or her salvation. AMEN

2

The Coming Kingship[1]

Text: Romans 8:1-2

There is therefore now no condemnaton for those who are in Christ Jesus. For the law of the Spirit of life in Christ Jesus has set you free from the law of sin and of death

THIS MORNING I WANT to follow up on last Sunday's theme of the "coming battle." After battles are over it is time to crown the new king. It is so in our world; it is similarly the case in God's plan of salvation. Another important Advent theme then is the "coming of the King."

We do not crown kings in America, thanks to George Washington, but we do elect and inaugurate presidents. We are in the midst of the process right now, so we have some idea of the importance of a prior commitment to the candidate who wins. Supporters of Ronald Reagen will get top jobs in Washington; Republican congressmen and congresswomen will get influential committee assignments and places of honor when lunching with him. The same happens in our own town after an election. Those supporting

---

1. Preached in the Covenant Church of Thomaston, CT, on December 9, 1984.

the wrong candidate find themselves out of a job, out of power, and probably out of an important lunch.

Ancient battles for kingship are even more decisive in the sense that winners win bigger and losers lose bigger. Not infrequently the latter pay for ill-chosen loyalty with their life. Adonijah found this out after Solomon became king, and so did others who supported Adonijah.

The rise of communism in Russia, China, and Cuba; of Nazi Socialism in Germany; and of militant Islam in Iran were all like ancient battles for kingship. And when the aspirants became victors they were ruthless in defeating their enemies. Violence continued when the victors defeated other enemies. The Russians entering Berlin in 1945 killed people immediately. I had a pastor friend in California who told me how close he came to death in April of that year. His father, because he had been in the German army, was captured by the Russians, sent off to prison, and died there. My friend Bill, who was only 9 years old, stood with his younger sister and their mother in a line of people about to be shot by Russian soldiers. Mother prayed while others cried loudly. Only because a bomb exploded in the building forcing the soldiers to flee did they have a chance to escape. And they did escape. It was the price you paid for being in the army of Adolf Hitler, a man who saw himself as messiah (or king) of the world. Those on the losing side were under condemnation. Much the same happened earlier in the Bolshevik Revolution in Russia, later in Mao's takeover in China, in Castro's takeover in Cuba, in Khomenei's takeover in Iran.

People sometimes think they can make decisions as they go along, choosing at the last moment which side to be on. This often works well, but not in the choosing of a king, when you must make your decision ahead of time. Dietrich Bonhoeffer, German pastor during World War II, made a decision early on against the messiah of Germany and for the Messiah of heaven, and while he suffered for his decision, he won the crown reserved for those who accept Jesus as Lord and King. When Bonhoeffer talked about the importance of prior commitment he compared it to boarding a train. He said boarding the right train or wrong train makes all the difference. If you board the wrong train there is nothing you can do when you learn it is going in the wrong direction. It is of no use whatever to run along the corridor in the opposite direction.

When Jesus was on earth he called for a commitment from people to follow him into his kingdom. It was a prior commitment, for he had not yet been proclaimed King of kings and Lord of lords. Some made the decision to follow him; others did not. So it is with us. We must decide ahead of time whether or we want Jesus to be Lord of our life. We may not have the opportunity to make a last minute decision before the crowning spoken of in Revelation. We need to do it now.

Those of you who have now joined the church, are you making a commitment to let Jesus be Lord and King in your life until he comes to reign forever? You are making your commitment before Jesus has been crowned; you have not seen the great battle that will end human history. None of us sitting here have. That is what being a person of faith is all about. We hope for what we have not seen. When you commit yourself to Jesus you commit yourself to the one who has the future in his hands. You have no worry about future punshment. Paul says, "There is therefore now no condemnation for those who are in Christ Jesus." Places of honor in the kingdom are reserved for you. AMEN

3

The Coming Order[1]

Text: Matthew 12:43–45

When the unclean spirit has gone out of a person, it wanders through waterless regions looking for a resting place, but it finds none. Then it says, 'I will return to my house from which I came.' When it comes, it finds it empty, swept, and put in order. Then it goes and brings along seven other spirits more evil than itself, and they enter and live there; and the last state of that person is worse than the first. So will it be also with this evil generation

I HAVE SPOKEN THE last two weeks about the battle and coming of a new king into power as the first of two great acts in God's coming. It happened in the past; it is happening in the present; it will happen in the future. The next great event in the sequence is the "new order," or "new creation." Battles leave things in chaos; usually they result in growing chaos. The new king must restore order and usher in a period of stability and creativity.

This sequence of events is seen not only in antiquity but also in modern times, in monarchies and dictatorships, also in

---

1. Preached on the Covenant Church of Thomaston, CT, on December 16, 1984.

democracies like our own. Four years ago our current President ran on the assertion that things in Washington were a mess. In the recent election he claimed that things were finally put in order, even though one candidate of the opposition said Washington was still in a mess. The charge of existing chaos is standard campaign rhetoric, and an aspiring leader must promise to restore order, bringing stability and creativity.

Looking into the Old Testament we find that the period of the Judges was very chaotic. Life when Samson was judge is example enough, especially if you look at what biblical passages are omitted in the Sunday School material. The last verse of Judges sums up the period: "In those days there was no king in Israel; all the people did what was right in their own eyes" (Judg 21:25).

The need was for a king who could bring order. The continual military threat caused people to ask for a king, and Samuel's sons, who might have succeeded him, were not behaving well as judges (1 Sam 8:1–3). So Saul was chosen. He was a fighter of reputation, having rescued the people of Jabesh-gilead from the barbaric Ammonites (1 Samuel 11). When he assumed power progress was made against these enemies as well as the Philistines who were pressing Israel on the west. Saul brought an order to Israel not present during the period of the Judges. He built a modest capital at Gibeah, a part of which can be seen today from excavations of the site. The erection of buildings is one mark of creative activity, and Saul ushered in a new creative period in Israel.

The same was repeated only more so when David became king. Under David the Philistine threat was eliminated; enemies to the east were brought in check; and greater order prevailed in the land. David built a large capital in Jerusalem. He also set in motion a new creative period, being himself a prolific psalm writer and increasing music in worship, even though as yet there was no temple. David wanted to build a temple, but Nathan the prophet told him the Lord did not want a temple (2 Samuel 7). David also assembled a large company of administrators and formed a government on the Egyptian model.

Solomon repeated the feat. If David won the peace, Solomon kept it. No wars of consequence occurred during his reign. Peace is another sign of stability and order. Many new buildings were built in Jerusalem, including a temple. Creative forces at work can also be seen in expanded trade during his reign. Solomon built a fleet of ships at the southern port of Ezion-geber from which they sailed to Orphir for gold (1 Kgs 9:26-28). Solomon was also a trader in horses and chariots (1 Kgs 10:28-29). And if David wrote many psalms, Solomon is said to have composed 3000 proverbs and 1005 songs (1 Kgs 4:32). It is also assumed that Solomon had a school in the temple or palace where scribes wrote history, love stories, and other works.

Kings of other nations followed the same course: fighting battles, assuming the kingship, creating a new order. They did the same when they conquered other nations. We have in our possession a text reporting what Sargon II of Assyria said about his conquest of Samaria in 722 B.C. From the Bible we hear only about the chaos accompanying the final days of the Northern Kingdom, but from Sargon we hear about how order was restored. The reconstructed text reads:

> At the begi[nning of my royal rule I . . . the town
> of the Sama]rians [I besieged, conquered]. . . [for the god . . .
> who le]t me acheve (this) my triumph . . . I led away as
> prisoners 27,290 inhabitants of it (and) [equipped] from
> among [them (soldiers to man)] 50 chariots for my royal
> corps . . . [The town I] re[built] better than (it was) before
> and [settled] therein people from countries which [I] myself
> [had con]quered. I placed an officer of mine as governor
> over them and imposed upon them tribute as (is customary)
> for Assyrian citizens.[2]

At the beginning of the Bible we are told how God created the world out of chaos. The earth was said to be "without form and void." Darkness covering the deep was a remnant of chaos. The "deep" (Gen 1:2) was the great fresh-water ocean under the earth

---

2. James B. Pritchard ed., *Ancient Near Eastern Texts*3 (Princeton: Princeton University Press, 1969), 284.

that ancients believed was a vestige of pre-creation chaos. When the Spirit of God took control of the forces of the deep, creation could begin. And it did begin.

At the end of the Bible we are given a similar message. There we are told that God will win his final victory over the chaos of this world, Jesus will be proclaimed King of kings and Lord of lords, and the new creation will begin. John in his vision gives us a preview of this new creation in Revelation 21. We know there will be an end of chaos, for verse 1 says that "the sea was no more." The sea is the last vestige of chaos, and John says it is gone. In the next verse is the unveiling of the New Jerusalem, which replaces the primordial Garden of Eden. This beautiful city comes down out of heaven filled with the saints, described as a bride adorned in brilliant splendor about to be presented to the groom, who is Jesus. Detail of the bridal array is like what we are accustomed to get from a newspaper society editor. There is also no temple in the city, for there is no longer need for one. God is there with the Lamb, who is Jesus.

We see then at the beginning of the Bible the new order that was. At the end is a preview of the new order to be. And within the Bible is announced the new order beginning for each person who has done battle with the forces of evil, who accepts Jesus as Lord and King, and who experiences the beginning of a new creation, replacing chaos in the former evil reign.

This brings me to my text. It comes from Matthew 12, which early in the chapter contains the story of a man for whom Jesus became Lord and Master. The text is a teaching following this dramatic event, showing how the coming of Jesus into a person's life brings order. The man brought to Jesus could neither speak nor hear. It is said that he possessed a demon. Jesus heals him, and the discussion following the healing centers around demon possession and the power Jesus has to cast out demons. Jesus compares himself to one who enters the house in which a strong man lives, ties up the strong man, and plunders the house (v 29).

I used to be troubled by this verse because I thought it depicted Jesus as a kind of robber, but that is not really so. The vivid image is to show that Jesus must do in an individual life what he did in Jerusalem when he entered the temple, overturned the tables, and chased out the money changers. In both cases he was confronting the forces of chaos and restoring order. With the man he chased out an unclean spirit and did some internal housecleaning. The person became like a house emptied of clutter, swept, and put in order (v 44).

I don't know how you feel about entering a house where everything is in disarray. Do you not prefer living yourself where there is order? I know differences exist. I have seen both, and so have you. There is a widespread myth that people living amidst disorder can nevertheless be organized. I don't believe it. Yes, I know people who on occasion can go directly to a pile of clutter and retrieve something, but I also know that often they cannot find what they are looking for, that they lose a great deal of things, and that they often do not know what is theirs and what belongs to their neighbor. Such people can be and usually are extremely inefficient. In any case, we see from our text that God comes out clearly on the side of order.

I have seen professors at the university who have books spread out on the desk when they are working, but everything else is in order. I have also entered the offices of colleagues where everything is a mess—desks piled high with mounds of papers, books all over the floor, chaos everywhere. Some office personnel also live in unbelievable clutter. When I was at Yale the man in charge of the keys and the mail was such a one. A myth circulated that he could nevertheless find anything. It was not true. What happened was that when he did manage to find something, it was so remarkable that people could not stop talking about it. Good stories are made of such things. A few weeks ago I received from his office two letters mailed from Europe over a year ago. They were somewhere in the mail room. I know this for certain: A person living amidst chaos cannot be creative. Creation is the opposite of chaos; creation can only come out of chaos, not the reverse; creation is a victory over chaos; creation reigns where there is order.

I would like to close with a warning that is also present in our text. It is important and must be heeded. We are told that an unclean spirit that has been expelled can come back with seven companions more worse than itself, and if they get entrance the last state of that person will become worse than the first. This is a sobering word for us Christians. When Jesus comes into our lives and becomes Lord and King he begins in us a new creation and sets up a new order. It is a beautiful thing. But if we fall back into chaotic living we end up in worse shape than the person who never let Christ into their heart. I have seen it happen, and it is tragic.

The message of Christmas is a message of peace resulting from what we have been talking about. Jesus came to a silent Bethlehem. We sing about it in our carol. In Jesus God came to end the din and chaos of war. Let us cherish the peace existing in our hearts, for the waters of chaos are ever near and wait to engulf us until that day when "the sea is no more." AMEN

4

The Coming God[1]

Text: John 1:1–15

In the beginning was the Word, and the Word was with God, and the Word was God. He was in the beginning with God. All things came into being through him, and without him not one thing came into being. What has come into being in him was life, and the life was the light of all people. The light shines in the darkness, and the darkness did not overcome it. There was a man sent from God, whose name was John. He came as a witness to testify to the light, so that all might believe through him. He himself was not the light, but he came to testify to the light. The true light, which enlightens everyone, was coming into the world. He was in the world, and the world came into being through him; yet the world did not know him. He came to what was his own, and his own people did not accept him. But to all who received him, who believed in his name, he gave power to become children of God, who were born, not of blood or of the will of the flesh or of the will of man, but of God. And the Word became flesh and lived among us, and we have seen his glory, the glory as of a father's only son, full of

---

1. Preached in the Covenant Church of Thomaston, CT, on December 23, 1984.

The Coming God

grace and truth. (John testified to him and cried out, "This was he of whom I said, 'He who comes after me ranks ahead of me because he was before me.'")

DURING ADVENT WE HAVE spoken thus far about a coming battle, a coming kingly rule, and a coming order. This morning I would like us to think about our "coming God." Certain Christian theologians are telling us today that our God is a God who "comes." What do they mean? One point they are trying to make is that the God we worship is not simply a God who was. The concern here is to recover the message of Revelation, which states that God was, is, and will be. Much Christian worship and practice is backward-looking, focusing on what happened in the past and much tied to ideas and ways of living that are out of date. Small wonder that young people get the idea that our God is not for them and the world they live in today.

The great truth that God has come in the person of Jesus may be of help here, since one who follows Jesus must always be living actively in the present, and should as well have sights set on the future. The Bible as a whole should get us to be more forward-looking, affirming as it does that God take the initiative with people, not always having to be sought out, even though seeking God is something we must do (Isa 55:6–7). The Israelites affirm time and again that God sought them out and that they were found. Christians ancient and modern affirm the same.

A comparison can be made here with Buddha, the great religious teacher of India who lived in about the sixth or fifth century B.C., someone every bit as important as Ghandi. The story of Buddha is one of a long and arduous search. Buddha gave up his royal estate, kissed a beautiful wife and child good-bye, and entered the forest in ragged attire where he spent six years searching for the light. He studied philosophy, fasted, and practiced other forms of human privation. He also developed powers of mystic concentration, having learned such from his Hindu teachers.

It is fascinating to read how illumination came to him:

You Are the Light of the World

> One evening near Gaya in northeast India, south of the current town of Patna, he sat beneath a fig tree which has since come to be known popularly as the Bo tree... Tradition reports that the Buddha, sensing that he was on the brink of enlightenment, seated himself that... evening with the vow not to rise until illumination was his.[2]

To be especially noted is the fierce determination the Buddha had to secure divine revelation. He sat down and would not get up until the light dawned. It is no wonder people of the world came to admire him; it is no wonder a religion grew up around him; he was determined as few are to find the light believed to transcend normal human perception.

When we go to the Bible we enter another world entirely. There God comes to Abraham, appearing almost by surprise in the person of messengers at the oaks of Mamre (Gen 18:1). How different is the Buddha's experience from calls issued by God to Moses, the prophets, and the Israelite people. Paul in his letter to the Romans quotes Isa 65:2, where God says, "I held out my hands all day long to a rebellious people" (Rom 10:21). How different from the angel of the Lord appearing to Mary telling her that she would bear the Savior of the world. How different, too, from the announcement of that birth to shepherds going about the ordinary work of keeping sheep.

The Bible has no comparable story about someone striving intensely for divine light, nor also like the Buddha who spent another 45 years not revealing the light, but pointing people in the direction of the light. The God of the Bible comes to men and women proclaiming a word to them. They are usually surprised, sometimes frightened, as was the case at Mount Sinai when the Lord appeared to people in a loud voice out of the fire, the cloud, and thick darkness. They were deathly afraid, and approached Moses saying:

---

2. Huston Smith, *The Religions of Man* (New York: Harper & Bros., 1958), 93.

> Look, the LORD our God has shown us his glory and greatness, and we have heard his voice out of the fire. Today we have seen that God may speak to someone and the person may still live. So now why should we die? For this great fire will consume us; if we hear the voice of the LORD our God any longer, we shall die. For who is there of all flesh that has heard the voice of the living God speaking out of fire, as we have, and remained alive? Go near, you yourself, and hear all that the LORD our God will say. Then tell us everything that the LORD our God tells you, and we will listen and do it (Deut 5:24–27)

John in our text for this morning says that the Word—which is also Light—came into the world at God's initiative. John the Baptist announced it before it came. The marvelous message of Christmas is that the Lord has come, come to us in the babe of Bethlehem. The prophets told of his coming long ago. No one had to sit under a tree and vow not to get up until the light shined. God comes when he comes, but he does come. Some are ready; some are not. Many are overcome with surprise. Today's message is no different. Revelation has these closing words from the risen Jesus: "Surely I come quickly," to which he adds, "Even so, come, Lord Jesus" (Rev 22:20 KJV).

Finally, a word about what we should do while waiting for his coming. The Bible says we are to wash our robes and get ready for the Heavenly Banquet. That great event is coming, and we must get cleaned up so as to be ready for it. Here again is another striking contrast with the noble Buddha. He prepared for finding the light by not washing himself for months. It is said that the dirt grew so thick upon his body that it fell off of its own accord. We know today of baseball, football, and basketball players, also players of other sports, who vow not to change their shirt, not to shave, not to shower until the victory is theirs. People generally live in a similar way when preparing for the future: letting dirt pile up; polluting water and air; throwing junk along the roadside; dispensing garbage on book racks at the checkout of grocery stores and on cable TV; and not a few at Christmas parties this year will be preparing for Hell instead of for Heaven.

In many and various ways we need to live for a God who will come. We may still seek this God, but need not go to extraordinary meaures to find him. More than this, he will come when we seek him and sometimes also when we do not. AMEN

5

The Coming Banquet[1]

Text: 1 Corinthians 11:23–32

For I received from the Lord what I also handed on to you, that the Lord Jesus on the night when he was betrayed took a loaf of bread, and when he had given thanks, he broke it and said, "This is my body that is for you. Do this in remembrance of me." In the same way he took the cup also, after supper, saying, "This cup is the new covenant in my blood. Do this as often as you drink it, in remembrance of me." For as often as you eat this bread and drink the cup, you proclaim the Lord's death until he comes. Whoever, therefore, eats the bread or drinks the cup of the Lord in an unworthy manner will be answerable for the body and blood of the Lord. Examine yourselves, and only then eat of the bread and drink of the cup. For all who eat and drink without discerning the body, eat and drink judgment against themselves. For this reason many of you are weak and ill, and some have died. But if we judged ourselves, we would not be judged. But when we are judged by the Lord, we are disciplined so that we may not be condemned along with the world

---

1. Preached in the Covenant Church of Hilmar, CA, on January 24, 1981.

You Are the Light of the World

I SHOULD LIKE TO conclude this series during Advent with the event culminating the salvation drama and inaugurating of the new age. This event is the divine banquet. In ancient times, and also today, the victory of battle, the crowning of the leader, and the establishment of a new order is brought to a climax with a banquet. We proceed this way in our nation, also in the church.

The banquet is the culmination of important events. It celebrates the beginning of a new reign. At the banquet one toasts the greatness of a new rule now dawning upon people. In the Christian community we speak of the banquet as we speak about all other events: the banquet that was, namely the Last Supper; the anticipated banquet celebrated in Holy Communion; and the banquet that will be, which is the Heavenly Banquet described in Revelation 21–22.

Occasions of eating and drinking, whether they be at large banquets or something on a smaller scale, are fragile in the sense that they can easily break apart and result in damage or destruction. I don't know the details of the party in Modesto that led to a man being caught at New Deal Market for shooting two men ostensibly his friends, killing one. But I know that eating and drinking go hand in hand with three evils: self-centeredness; inequalities between people; and friction of one kind or another.

When we were living in Beirut some years ago two Arab men were having breakfast one morning; they were said to be friends. When they finished eating the one offered to pay for the breakfasts. The other objected, saying he would pay. It was a classic case of honor among Arabs, with each being insulted by the other wanting to pay the bill. Well, a fight ensued, and the one after getting up from the floor went the short distance to his home, returned with a gun, and shot the other man dead. Prosecution in the courts became bogged down because it was a dispute over honor. I don't know what the final outcome was.

Generosity in this case was largely self-centeredness. The result was friction, and in the end there was tragedy. Inequality can also cause friction. This happens when one eats too much and another gets nothing. It can happen if one gets a larger piece of pie at the restaurant than others at the table. I became concerned last week at the beginning of our vacation, which was spent with my wife's sister and her family, because her sister in doing the shopping and did not buy the kind of food we wanted. I suggested that Linda should have done the shopping.

You will remember that at the Last Supper self-centeredness came out in the open when an argument broke out among the disciples about who was the greatest. Here at Corinth is also self-centeredness and inequality causing friction at the celebration of the Lord's Supper. People are not waiting for one another; some are eating too much while others are going hungry. We know from another part of Paul's letter that this church was riddled with competing factions (1 Cor 3:1–9).

Paul therefore has to remind people of the Last Supper as Jesus conceived it to be. Eating and drinking should begin with a prayer thanking God; eating and drinking should be a social time, a time for give and take, for building one another up, not for self-centeredness; eating and drinking should eliminate inequalities, not create them; eating and drinking should be a time for healing, not friction and things sometimes much worse.

Begin eating and drinking with prayer. We do this in our celebration of communion. But if eating at the Lord's table is to be a model for other eating, as it has long been for Christian people, should we not begin meals at home with prayer? Many have forgotten this common courtesy to God. Prayer also brings people together as they sit around the table.

Eating and drinking should be a social time. In our current celebration of communion we do not have an opportunity for being social, other than sitting together or going to the communion rail together. In the early church there was an agape feast, which was more social in nature. I would like to see communion incorporated into a larger meal with people sitting at tables. As it is, church life becomes a private version of the social time we experience at home, although today even in our homes people are finding food for themselves and eating alone. The problem in Corinth was different. People were bringing their own food from home and eating it at church, and they were inconsiderate, not regarding those around them who had less food or no food at all.

Eating and drinking should eliminate inequalities. The church should be a place where those who have help those who have less. In our communion service there is no problem of inequality due to the way things are set up. But what about at home? Is there a "pecking order" around your table, or do you see to it that everyone—guest, as well as children—is treated with fairness? Do you pass food around, or just leave it in front of where you are sitting? Table fellowship should be a time of equality and fairness in the distribution of food and drink.

Eating and drinking should be happy times, times of healing and not times of friction. How often have you sat around the table at some holiday feast only to have an argument break out between family members? It is not an isolated occurrence. As for our communion celebration in church, it is a time for self-examination and resolving to work at healing some sore point between you and another brother or sister in the fellowship. In Rev 22:2 the tree of life remerges at the Heavenly Banquet (cf. Gen 2:9). Its leaves are for the healing of the nations. Our meal this morning is a preparation for that grand meal of the future. AMEN

Christmas

6

Room for Jesus[1]

Text: Luke 2:7

And she gave birth to a son, her first-born. She wrapped him in swaddling clothes, and laid him in a manger, because there was no room for them to lodge in the house

HISTORIANS SAY HISTORY MUST be written anew in each generation. Nevertheless, traditions survive the coming and going of many generations, and new ways of looking at ancient events come only infrequently. Yet they do come.

The birth of Jesus is viewed differently today than at earlier times. According to the typical Christmas pageant, which builds on centuries of tradition, Mary and Joseph arrive in Bethlehem late at night. They seek lodging at an inn along the road. They are turned away because the inn is full, although in our pageant this year the poem by Myles Connolly has the inkeeper rejecting them because they are poor. Mary and Joseph then go to one or two other inns, but they too are full. Looking further, they finally locate a stable either adjacent to the last inn or somewhere else, and there they settle in for the night. During the night the baby is born. No one is present in this forlorn place except Mary, Joseph,

---

1. Preached in the Covenant Church of Hilmar, CA, on December 24, 1980.

and some animals. The baby is wrapped in peasant cloths and laid in a manger. Later that evening shepherds come to visit. Later still, at the same location, three wisemen from the east come bringing gifts to the baby after following a star that settled over the place where the baby lay.

This is the basic script. There are, of course, songs, poems, and Christmas pageants that alter details, or get things mixed up, e.g., in Evie Tornquist's Christmas record where she sings about shepherds seeing a star. But I am not referring to obvious errors of this kind. The typical pageant interprets the biblical story from the accounts in Luke 2 and Matthew 2, and fills in the details as best it can.

The most ancient tradition known to us dates from the second century A.D. Justin Martyr gives this account of Jesus' birth: Mary and Joseph arrive in Bethlehem; Joseph cannot find lodging in the town so they take up quarters in a cave outside of town. While there, i.e., after a few days, Mary gives birth to Jesus in the cave. The baby is laid in a manger, which means animals are there. Here the wise men find the family. Justin makes no mention of shepherds. The tradition of Jesus being born in a cave became well-established, so that by A.D. 325 the Church of the Nativity was built over caves in Bethlehem. You can see them today when you visit the church. One will note also that in Roman Catholic creches the Holy Family appear in a cave.

Today we are becoming conscious that traditions expand upon what is recorded in the Bible and do not always present things just as the Bible states. Also, biblical accounts are open to different interpretations, and while our generation reads the same or similar Bibles, it reads the text differently than former generations. For example, when the RSV came out 25–30 years ago, we learned when doing our Christmas pageant not to say, "Wonderful, Counselor," but "Wonderful Counselor" from Isa 9:6. The RSV also had "swaddling cloths" instead of "swaddling clothes" in Luke 2:7, which was largely a change to more current English. The NRSV has "bands of cloth."

We also realize that the Bible makes no mention of there being three wise men. We had four on Sunday evening, and one was a woman! We also do not know whether they came to the manger or later to some other location. In Matt 2:11 it says that the wise men went into a "house" to see the baby Jesus.

Biblical scholars taking a fresh look at Luke 2:7 have sharpened the picture considerably, enough so that it may mean our Christmas pageants will have to be rewritten a bit. The Greek word translated "inn" (κατάλυμα) is misleading. I read the NEB translation this morning, which has "house." The Greek word means "place of lodging," and while such a place could be a caravan stop along the road (a khan), it could also be "guest room" in a house, the meaning it has in Luke 22:11, where it refers to the room where Jesus ate the Last Supper with his disciples. Most likely this is the meaning the term has in the Christmas story.

What we are talking about is a house with a guest room, common in Palestine before the days of inns, hotels, and motels, and common today in all parts of Europe. The "Fremdenzimmer" in Germany is a guest room in the house for travelers. Linda and I stayed in one in Germany. We should therefore read Luke 2:7 as follows: "And she gave birth to her firstborn son and wrapped him in swaddling cloths, and laid him in a manger because there was no place for them in the guest room." This may have a strange ring to our ears, but it would make perfectly good sense to an ancient Palestinian familiar with the layout of a typical house.

Let me explain. This house in Bethlehem, like many houses today, would contain one large room where the family lives. The living area rises about four feet above ground level. At one end of the house animals are housed on ground level; they are not kept in separate stables. They are brought into the house at night and then led out in the morning. People in this part of the world have no aversion to being with the animals; in fact, they like it and want it this way. Body heat of the animals provides warmth for people in the house and there is less danger of them being stolen.

Mangers were commonly built into the area between the raised family room and the animal quarters, acting as a kind of divider. They would therefore be a safe place for a new baby to be laid if a cradle was unavailable. Thus when Luke says that they laid the baby in the manger the ancient reader knows immediately where Mary and Joseph are: they are in the family room. Why are they not in the guest room? Because it is occupied; others are already there.

Let us then tell the story anew. It is the same story with just some details brought into clearer focus. Mary and Joseph arrive in Bethlehem for the census. Mary is pregnant, and they need to find a suitable place should she have her baby. Bethlehem has no commercial inns, which exist only on major Roman roads between towns, and no major Roman road goes to Bethlehem. Since Joseph is of the house of David, he will be a welcome guest in town. He will likely have relatives there, but if not, someone else will take him in, especially if his wife is pregnant. The home village is an integral part of a person's identity, and even if Joseph were not born there, he need only appear at the home of some kin, recite his geneology, and he is among friends. He will say, "I am Joseph, son of Jacob, son of Mattan, son of Eleazar, son of Eliud," and the immediate response will be, "You are welcome, what can we do for you?"

Joseph thus finds a house in which they can lodge. The house has a guest room, but it is occupied. Other family may be there, perhaps also for the census. But Mary and Joseph can stay with the family in the main living area. From our point of view it will seem crowded and lacking in privacy, but by ancient Near Eastern standards this will present no problem; it will be snug and comfortable. While there, Mary delivers. Since they were staying in the family room, the manger was a convenient place to lay the newborn. (We have laid our small children in playpens in the living room with pillows and blankets for protection).

People are on hand to help, probably a number of people. The men will sit separately while the women help with the birth. Swaddling cloths are not old rags, but special wrappings. We have records of kings being wrapped in them (Wisdom 7:4–5). They will be like a homemade grandma quilt. Shepherds, at the bottom of the social ladder and whom some rabbis declared to be unclean, will have no fear in seeking out this ordinary house where the baby lies in a manger. They may have to knock on a few doors to find the right house, but they will find it. Wise men come later, but maybe not much later, since Matthew has Mary and Joseph still in a Bethlehem house.

What meaning can we get from all this? One point should be clear: there was room for Jesus! Luke says another lodging area was filled, but that was not his main point. His point is that a place was found when the Savior was born—a place in a simple home; a place filled with people who could share the joy of the baby's coming; a place where shepherds from outside the village could come and extend their welcome. Luke is not saying anything about inhospitality. His message is just the opposite: Jesus is given a royal welcome by simple folk at the time of his coming. If this be the good news of Christmas, and I believe it is, should not each and every one of us open our homes and hearts to him this night? Let there be room for Jesus in our town as there was in Bethlehem those many years ago. AMEN

Prayer Week

7

"Our Father in Heaven, Hallowed Be Your Name"[1]

Text: Matthew 6:9

Pray then in this way: Our Father in heaven, hallowed be your name

IN THE NEW YEAR we commonly pause as Christians to reflect on the importance of prayer, and set aside special times to pray. We have our own cottage prayer meetings as they have come to be called, and this past week at Bethel Lutheran was a service in the Week of Prayer for Christian Unity. Have we also been praying more on our own?

I would like to focus today and in the next few Sundays on the most beloved of prayers—the Lord's Prayer. We know it well; we say it in worship every Sunday, reason enough, I suppose, why we should stop once and a while and reflect on its words. When we get in the habit of saying anything words have a tendency to lose their meaning, and we do not know what we are saying.

The Lord's Prayer is included in Matthew's Sermon on the Mount, but it appears also in Luke's gospel (Luke 11:2–4), where

1. Preached in the Covenant Church of Menominee, MI, on January 24, 1993.

it is shorter. Luke, however, gives us the occasion that led to the prayer being given. Jesus had just concluded a prayer of his own, and one of his disciples said to him, "Lord, teach us to pray, as John taught his disciples."

It was common for teachers to give disciples instruction when they were off by themselves. Rabbis, and other religious teachers, would teach them prayers. Disciples of John the Baptist may have been taught a number of prayers by him. The Pharisees taught prayers and so did Essene Jews living near the Dead Sea. Some were committed to memory, just as today the Lord's Prayer is memorized.

This morning I want to focus attention on the first petition of Jesus' prayer:

> Our Father in heaven
> Hallowed be your name

The disciples are told to address God in the way Jesus does, using the title "Father." Father is established usage for God in the OT, but it is still rare (14 times). The Canaanite god El was called "father," and perhaps for this reason Israelites shied away from using the term. But Jesus uses it often, especially when he prays. In parables he likens God to a master, a judge, a householder, a property owner, etc., but in prayers he seems to prefer "Father."

The Christian Church has used the term down through the ages. Only in the present day is it being challenged by the feminists. Mary Daly of Boston College has written a book entitled, *Beyond God the Father*. Others want to use "she" for God. At Harvard and Yale students have rewritten hymns for chapel use. John Greenleaf Whittier's "Dear Lord and Father of Mankind" has become "Dear Mother-Father of us all." The first petition of the Lord's Prayer, in a similar manner, has become, "Our Mother" or "Our Parent."

We therefore have thrust upon us a question unthinkable 25 years ago, namely, can we continue speaking of God as Father? Can we continue to pray, "Our Father?" It should be pointed out that some who object to the use of Father as a term for God are striking at ideas in error to begin with, e.g., that God is man, or male. Though the Bible uses primarily male images and male pronouns for God, it also states that God is not man (Hos 11:9 RSV). We are also told that God comforts as a mother does her children (Isa 66:13).

What we are talking about are metaphors used as pointers to God, also other figures (similes, comparisons, etc.) used to describe what God is like. But even the boldest metaphor will not tell us what God is like. The essence of God lies hidden in mystery. Beyond all metaphors and revelations, hidden entirely from our view, is GOD. Beyond God the Father is not God the Mother, but the One, and only One, who transcends every finite category—GOD!

So can we continue to use Father for God? Of course we can! The Bible uses it; Jesus uses it; and it is used even though a multitude of other terms are available. I imagine we will probably see the rewriting of hymns for some time to come, but I do not expect a rewriting of the Bible. Even the NRSV was careful at this point in using inclusive language; so also the REB. Both tried to stay within limits imposed by the Hebrew and Greek.

There are other good reasons, I believe, why Father continues to be a perfectly good metaphor for God. Once we get past the notion that God is our father in a literal sense—which would sink us back into paganism because earthly fathers could then become gods—we can get on with being more positive about these words beginning the Lord's Prayer.

First of all, "father" is a personal metaphor, and we need to pray to a God who relates to us in a personal way. God is one who sees, hears, feels deeply, extends a helping hand and a strong arm of defense, and maybe also gets red and fiery in the nose when he is angry (In the OT the nose shows anger).

God in the Bible is also spoken of as a Spirit (=Wind), another good metaphor. We need to acknowledge God's invisible nature, his movement (cf. John 3:8), and his power. Spirit (or Wind) conveys these mysteries about God.

I want also a God who loves, and spirits (or winds) do not love. They are angry during storms; they are helpful in pushing sailboats across the water, but they do not love. They are not gracious and merciful. They are not righteous and just. They do not keep promises as fathers do. So while I am glad the Bible talks about God as a Spirit, I am also glad God is depicted as a Father. There are, of course, human fathers who do none of what I just mentioned, but that does not render invalid fathers who do—fathers who are personal, showing their children love, grace, mercy, fairness, faithfulness, etc.

Secondly, I am helped by the idea of God as Father because a father is a one who stands above me and has authority over me. We are God's children, and because of this we would do well to remember that God is someone whose dominance over us should never be open to question. Everyone—human fathers and reverend fathers—must look to the Father who is in heaven.

When the Fatherhood of God is lost sight of, we see tragedies occurring on an enormous scale, such as the one in San Francisco and Jonestown some years back—a scene doubtless to be etched in our minds for years to come. The man Jim Jones became the ultimate father—in his own eyes and in the eyes of those who followed him. I remember passing by People's Temple in San Francisco during Jim Jones' heyday. I worked just a few blocks away at the Bank of America. I remember too, as no doubt many of you do, the tragedy later occurring at Jonestown and the shock waves this sent through all of us, particularly those who were directly affected.

Shortly after the mass suicide in Guyana a note came across my desk, written by the Rev. John Moore, pastor of the First Methodist Church in Reno. He and his wife were touched by this tragedy because two of their daughters and one grandson were members of People's Temple, and were presumed to have died at Jonestown. In a sermon preached by the Rev. Moore the Sunday following the mass suicide, he wondered what had gone wrong. "What happened," he said, "to turn the dream which Mr. Jones had for helping the poor achieve justice into a virtual nightmare?" Two things, he believed, were wrong from the beginning: 1) Jim Jones had a touch of paranoia; and 2) worship taking place in his group was idolatrous. I quote from his comments about idolatry:

"Our Father in Heaven, Hallowed Be Your Name"

> The adulation and worship Jim Jones' followers gave him was idolatrous. We (i.e., me and my wife) expressed our concern from the first . . . Our children and members of People's Temple placed in Jim Jones the trust, and gave him the loyalty, that we were created to give God alone. To believe the First Commandment . . . affirms that every ideal and principle, every leader and institution, all morals and values, all means and ends, are subordinate to God. This means that they are all subject to criticism. There was no place for this criticism in People's Temple

This is but another way of saying that for members of People's Temple God was not Father. The father of fathers was Jim Jones. He was the authority above which there was no other. In praying to God as Father we acknowledge his authority over us. We pray as his children, which is how it should be between God and us.

The third reason I want to hold on to the Fatherhood of God is that fathers, because of who they are in relation to their children, are special people. This helps in understanding the second line of the petition, which tells us to keep God's name holy. Fathers are special simply because they are our fathers. Good fathers, of course, are always special people in the eyes of their children. I think of my own father, who was a good man, and in my eyes like no other man. I could say the same of my grandfather. But even more surprising is that fathers not particularly good are also taken to be special. Again and again I have discovered that woefully inadequate fathers still have a special place in the hearts of their children. I have found this to be true of fathers who have left home, fathers who come home drunk much of the time, even fathers who abuse their children.

Fathers—like mothers—have a creative function in the lives of their children, and nothing can alter this fact. This is why the Bible teaches that you are never to curse your parents. The Bible does not say, "Honor your father and mother only if they are good." Or, "Do not curse them unless they are bad." Even if they are unspeakably bad, children must not curse them. To curse your father or mother is to curse yourself. You owe your life to them.

God is a good and special Father because he created and redeemed us. To Israel was said:

> Is not he your father, who created you
> who made you and established you?
> Deut 32:6

> Have we not all one Father?
> Has not one God created us?
> Mal 2:10

Both creation and redemption are mentioned in our Old Testament lesson from Isaiah 43:

> But now thus says the LORD
> he who created you, O Jacob
> he who formed you, O Israel:
> Do not fear, for I have redeemed you
> I have called you by name, you are mine.
> Isa 43:1

In this beautiful passage God goes on to describe how, as Father, he protects his people—walking them through the water and the fire. He calls himself "the Holy One of Israel" (v 3). God is holy and his name is holy. His name, therefore, must not be taken in vain. We affirm the holiness of God every time we say: "Our Father in heaven, hallowed be your name." To pray "our Father" is also to affirm that we are his children. Paul had it right:

> When we cry "Abba! Father!" it is that very Spirit
> bearing witness with our spirit that we are children
> of God (Rom 8:15b-16). AMEN

8

"Your Kingdom Come, Your Will Be Done"[1]

Text: Matthew 6:10

Your kingdom come, your will be done, on earth as it is in heaven

THIS SECOND PETITION OF the Lord's Prayer contains two affirmations, "your kingdom come" and "your will be done," which mean about the same thing. To pray for the coming of God's kingdom is to pray for the coming of God's rule. And with God's rule comes an exercise of God's will. These are words people address to someone they want to be king.

In the Old Testament people came to Gideon and said,

> "Rule over us, you and your son and your
> grandson also; for you have delivered us out
> of the hand of Midian" (Judg 8:22)

But Gideon refused, saying the Lord must rule the people.

A monarchy, however, was later established in Israel. Samuel objected, but his protestations went unheeded. It seems his sons

---

[1]. Preached in the Covenant Church of Menominee, MI, on January 31, 1993.

were no better suited to be judges than were the sons of Eli suited to be priests. Samuel's sons, we are told, took bribes and perverted justice (1 Sam 8:3). So the Lord agreed to having a king in Israel, although he hastened to point out that the people were rejecting him as King.

Years later the kingdom of God came in all its glory to the prophet Isaiah while worshiping in the temple. He says,

> In the year that King Uzziah died, I saw the
> Lord sitting on a throne, high and lofty, and the
> hem of his robe filled the temple (Isa 6:1)

The words are heavy with meaning. Isaiah sees the Lord as King precisely when a king of Judah dies and everyone awaits a new king to ascend the throne. One might have expected Isaiah to say: "In the year that King Uzziah died I saw Jotham sitting on a throne, high and lofty . . . (cf. 2 Kings 15:32).

But for Isaiah the death of Uzziah was the occasion for the Lord becoming King. One imagines a stirring moment in the life of this young man. Up until this time Isaiah may not have acknowledged the Lord as sovereign—either in his own life or in the life of the nation. But when he does, uncleanness both in him and in his nation overwhelms him, and he says:

> "Woe is me! I am lost, for I am a man of
> unclean lips, and I live among a people
> of unclean lips . . ." (Isa 6:5)

A seraph then comes with a coal from the fire and touches his lips, and his sin and guilt are taken away. Isaiah hadn't prayed "your kingdom come," but the Lord's kingdom for him had nevertheless dawned. The Lord's will was also done, for not only was Isaiah cleansed, he was now placed into service as the Lord's messenger. Isaiah was willing. When the Lord asked who will go, he stepped forward and said, "Here am I; send me."

Note that the coming of God's rule and the exercising of God's will are both asked for on earth. It is not necessary to pray that these will happen in heaven. God is already sovereign in heaven. What God wants, and what we need, is for God to become sovereign

"Your Kingdom Come, Your Will Be Done"

on earth, that he be accepted by you, me, and all people as King instead of any other person or power that would rule us—some we may ourselves put on thrones because of a bent towards idolatry.

Today is reason for apprehension, at least, about the new President in our land, and I say this carefully knowing that idolatry can exist elsewhere than in the Oval Office. Idols in our land are legion. Besides sport superstars and video stars, mindless squandering of money on schemes to become rich, fascination with pleasures that even fools know will give way to an unhappy Monday morning, are the more subtle idols of houses, land, possessions, parents, children, and oneself that lead to every other idolatry. Whatever controls you ultimately is king in your life.

I have reflected much on the rule of God and the exercise of God's will in human affairs—perhaps more than any other facet of the Christian faith—and while I cannot say that I am anywhere near a full understanding of this mystery, I have, nevertheless, thoughts I would like to share. A sign some years back in front of a New Haven church read: "We must speak with a humility commensurate to our limited perspective, but we must speak!"

First, there are wills on earth opposed to God. Some are deliberately opposed; many more are opposed without a knowing of the opposition. I am sure many of the false prophets in the OT would have been utterly offended to have been called false prophets. So, too, many ministers and other Christians today if track was kept of ill-advised things they said and did. Peter, on one occasion was found to be on the side of Satan rather than of God (Mark 8:33). Paul discovered an opposing will deep within himself that was sin (Rom 7:14–20). It should not surprise us—although it should sober us—to learn that from time to time we will things that God would never think of us willing. A natural extension of our prayer might well be, "Let your will be mine, O God." Opposition is here on earth, not in heaven.

Some have suggested that there is more than one will of God. They talk about his "primary or absolute will" and his "permissive will." Those having gone through grief experiences will frequently cling to such an idea, for they feel that while God did not want their loved one to die, he nevertheless permitted it. That God experiences genuine hurt over what happens on earth I have no doubt. At the same time I do not think we can talk meaningfully about God having two wills. It is much better to think of God as having one will, and simply recognize that there is much about this one will we do not understand.

Secondly, and this follows on what we have just said about one will, we need to think of God's will being worked out in terms broader than our own will being worked out. We say, "God's will is not our will," and that is true. But it is true not simply because God disagrees with our will, but because his will is broader. This is the case with any king, any president, any leader having responsibility over large numbers of people. In every church I have served as pastor people have said to me, "I know you can't please everyone." What must it be like to be king? Or president?

The rub is when someone thinks their will should be everyone's will. To pray "your will be done" is to give God the space God needs to be God, the Sovereign One, the giver of life and health and taker of the same. God the Creator is also God the Reaper. Your God and my God is God of the world, God everlasting!

I believe God is concerned about each and every person. I also believe that he is concerned about small things in our lives and big things of this world. At the same time I am fully convinced that it is futile—indeed it reflects an over-evaluation of our individual worth—to look for every detail in one's life as fitting into God's plan. This sounds good, for it supports the idea of an extraordinary God who is all-knowing, all-powerful, everywhere present, etc. But when we think in these terms it is more likely that we are assuming we are at the center of God's universe, that everyone else and everything else is in orbit around us.

Not quite. God's will has to be understood in broader terms. He is never this partial to anyone. He is working out a plan for the world, for all generations, where some have a greater part to play, some a smaller part; some are closer to the center of his will, some farther away; some things do have importance, other things do not; some small things fit in, other big things do not.

"Your Kingdom Come, Your Will Be Done"

Scripture says that "in everything God works for good . . . " (Rom 8:28 RSV), which is better in my view than "all things work together for good" (KJV; NRSV). The whole point is that in suffering and weakness, which is what Paul has just talked about, God works for good. Paul does not mean that every single thing has a purpose in God's will.

When General Eisenhower planned to land allied forces in Europe on June 6, 1944, he had one will, which was to win the war and save lives. Yet he knew the assault would cost him lives—many lives. His will could not be understood in terms of one soldier's life—important as that might be—but in terms of the entire army and the entire effort of allied forces to win the war.

The passing of time usually, and the coming into maturity always, puts things in better perspective. Children think the world revolves around them. Adults in their prime may feel the same way, but the older and more mature we get the more we realize that we are not as important as we thought, and not everything we do or have done is God's will. The estimation of our own worth diminishes with age, and that is something I believe God does will!

Finally, God's will works out not on straight highways but on crooked paths. I just received a letter this past week giving me the following message: "I wish you well . . . on a road full of twists and turns which conceal the destination. God's blessing on the way." How much more is it true in the great march of human events. Only after time has passed do we see how crooked was our journey. At the time the flow was perhaps going in a different direction.

We must also never think that just because something happens it is the will of God. Ambitious people think in these terms, figuring that if they are quick enough to pull something off God has to sanction it. That is a subtle trap of the Devil. One can never equate "what is" or "what happens" with what God wills. Nor can we be fooled by those who always say, "You can't argue with success." Sometimes you have to argue with success. Many, many things succeed—yet only for a time—that are not God's will. God can use success to test us, as he did in Israel with false prophets who were able to perform miracles (Deut 13:1–5).

People flourish—again only for a time—outside God's will. Jeremiah gets very distraught over this, and cries in one of his confessions: "Why does the way of the guilty prosper? Why do all who are treacherous thrive?" (Jer 12:1).

One thing to remember is that present trends do not always continue. Thank God they do not! What is more, there are surprises in store for those who believe in a single will of God and his rule on earth. That is what twists and turns in the road are all about. And that is what makes praying for God's will to be done so exciting. Life may not be all you hoped for. It may be more! AMEN

9

"Give Us This Day Our Daily Bread"[1]

Text: Matthew 6:11

Give us this day our daily bread

THIS PETITION IS THE briefest in the Lord's Prayer—just one line instead of two or three. It is located at the center, which may account for its brevity. Here it provides the prayer balance and rhythm, which may not seem important, but could be for committing it to memory. The focus thus far has been on God. Now the focus shifts to us. We are to pray for bread, our most basic need.

The sequence followed thus far in the prayer is in one sense important, and in another sense not. It is important to focus first on God. We owe God what we owe anyone to whom we come with a request: courtesy and respect. We are children of the Heavenly Father, another reason why it is right to show respect. Children having learned to respect parents and others to whom they are beholden have learned a big lesson.

It is not important, however, to say "your will be done" before praying for a specific need. Looking at another important prayer

---

1. Preached in the Covenant Church of Menominee, MI, on February 7, 1993.

in the Bible, the one Jesus prayed in the Garden of Gethsemane, we find both elements present only they are reversed:

> "My Father, if it is possible, let this cup
> pass from me; yet not what I want but what you
> want (Matt 26:39)

The request that the cup pass comes first; concession to the divine will comes second. The main thing is that the two are kept together. It is not a good prayer if we pray only for what we want, nor also if we say simply, "your will be done." A complete prayer should contain both: a specific request, and a concession that God have final say. Praying simply "your will be done" is too ambiguous because it asks for nothing. What is more, if we pray this way we never know whether God has or has not answered. Prayers should ask for something, and the clearer the request the better.

Give us this day our daily bread. What does it mean? On one level the meaning is clear. Bread is primary sustenance for life—we see it more in undeveloped countries than in our own. Bread is basic in the Near East; also in Africa. I remember my friend in East Berlin telling me, now over 10 years ago, how he was supplying his father, who was a baker, with bread in a small town to the south where there was a shortage. Berlin had more bread than other cities. God only knows how many people today are praying for bread.

We must, however, give "bread" the broader meaning it possesses. Some people use it to mean money, e.g., "I've got to make some bread." In the Old Testament Hebrew *lhm* may mean a circular of baked bread (made from wheat flour); a cake of bread (made from barley); meat (a meaning it has also in Arabic); or food in general. It can even mean a feast. When God's messengers come to Abraham at the oaks of Mamre, he asks them to stay, wash their feet, and while refreshing themselves under a tree he will bring them "a little bread" (Gen 18:5). What does Abraham do? Well, for starters, he asks Sarah to make some cakes. Then he has a calf taken from the herd, gives it to a servant to prepare, and goes to get curds and milk for his guests. What we have is an oriental feast.

"Give Us This Day Our Daily Bread"

Staying for bread at Abraham's tent is like being served "coffee" at the home of some Swedish ladies I know.

Jesus intended an even broader meaning for bread when telling his disciples to pray for daily bread. For him bread meant more than food. We recall in the Garden of Gethsemane when Jesus asked if the "cup" might be kept from him, he was not thinking simply of the cup of wine given to condemned men before they died, but of the entire ordeal of suffering and death. We can thus broaden the meaning of bread to include all the supports of life: food, love and care, help and advice—in a word fellowship, leading to general well-being. When we pray to God for daily bread we are asking for fellowship that goes along with food. Food tastes better when people are sitting around the table eating it with you. God knows this, and therefore wants us to pray for fellowship, support, and sustenance in the broadest of terms. Why then do we not ask God for the sustenance we need? The two are related.

I have discovered that some people, indeed many, do not like making requests of others: They hate picking up the phone and calling for help; they hate asking people for anything in person; they hate bothering someone for bread; they hate asking for help of any kind. People going to the hospital hate to bother the pastor about their having to go. Perhaps, then, if we are unwilling to make requests of others, we may not want to make requests—even serious requests—to God. Do we really want to ask God for daily bread?

Maybe this is pride going along with our desire for independence. We want to take care of ourselves and do things for ourselves. An admirable trait, really. Handling one's own affairs is using the resources God has given us. Moreover, when we are self-sufficient we are not a burden to others. How glad I am for resourceful people wanting not to overburden themselves on others. If they can do things for ourselves they should do them. Praying for bread is one thing if no bread is available, but it is quite another if one will not go down to the store to get bread that is there, or will not work to have money to buy bread.

There are those, of course, who will point to Scripture where it talks about God taking care of the sparrows, as if hard work in life is unnecessary. But a wise biblical scholar from Great Britain pointed out some years ago that while it is true God takes care of the sparrows, it is also true that sparrows work hard for a day's food. Watch them sometime. Another wise teacher, this one an Arab from the Middle Ages, Ibrahim Khawwas, gave his disciples this maxim: "Allow what is done for you to be done for you; do for yourself that which you have to do for yourself." We say, do we not, that "God helps those who help themselves."

At the same time, or perhaps in the spirit of these proverbs, we know there are times we do need help, also that many things in life cannot be accomplished without a team effort. It does not mean we are incapable. It means we cannot do everything by ourselves, and that sometimes, however much we wish it weren't so, we come up weak instead of strong. Relying on others may also teach us to rely upon God. God sought with manna in the wilderness to teach Israel dependence upon him, perhaps also of their need to work together so everyone would have anough to eat. It says, "But when they measured it with an omer, those who gathered much had nothing over, and those who gathered little had no shortage" (Exod 16:18). This sounds like when we used to go blueberry picking years ago in Wisconsin. I never got much in my pail—sometimes it would tip over and I would lose some of what I had, but others made up for my lack, and that evening we had more than enough for blueberry pie and Swedish blueberry kräm.

In our prayer life we come to realize that we cannot do everything ourselves. Many things require a team effort—at home, at church, at work, in the community. To pray for daily bread is to pray for life in its fullness. In the world's wisdom strength is good and weakness is bad. But in the economy of God both can be for the good. The Lord told Paul while he was in prayer: "for (my) power is made perfect in weakness" (2 Cor 12:9). We may be too timid to ask for bread because we are fearful or maybe afraid of being turned down. Mixed in with human pride is timidity.

"Give Us This Day Our Daily Bread"

Linda and I went to the local Chinese restaurant a couple weeks ago not knowing it was Chinese New Year. The place was crowded, and it looked like it might be quite a while before getting seated. The hostess told us, however, that if we would join up with someone else we could get a table more quickly, as there were more larger tables than small ones. Well, it happened that a neighboring pastor was also waiting with his wife and daughter to be seated. We had said hello to them when we came in. I wondered if we should ask them to join us. But maybe we would rather have a table by ourselves. Would they like to join us? Maybe they would also rather have a table by themselves. I hesitated, but decided to ask them. They said, "Sure," and we took a large table together. That evening we had more than food; we had fellowship and a chance to better know our neighbors and co-workers in ministry. But some timidity had to be overcome.

To ask for daily bread, finally, is to ask for Jesus, who is the bread of God from heaven come to give life to the world. From our NT Lesson we learn that there is more to being fed ordinary bread—even bread extraordinarily multiplied. If Jesus wants us to pray for bread, food, fellowship, and care, he wants even more for us to pray that he come into our lives. He gives water that will never make us thirsty again; he also gives bread that will no longer make us hungry.

We approach the Lord's table this morning, partaking again of the bread that is the body of our Lord, broken for us, that we might have life eternal. If there is anyone here who is hungry this morning, make your hunger known to God; make it known to one of us. People here have bread on their tables that they can share; people here can provide you with fellowship if you need it; people here can lead you to Jesus if you do not yet know him. AMEN

10

"Forgive Us Our Debts"[1]

Text: Matthew 6:12

And forgive us our debts, as we also have forgiven our debtors

THROUGHOUT THIS SERIES I have been stressing the importance of taking the Lord's prayer as a unity, keeping petitions together that belong together, and seeing how one petition ties in with the next. Here in the fourth petition two parts must also not be separated: "And forgive us our debts, as we also have forgiven our debtors." Forgiveness we ask of God is tied in with forgiveness we grant to others. Or put another way, communication with heaven ties in with communication occurring on earth.

Again we can say that sequence is important in one sense, and in another not important. Although we pray first that God will forgive us our debts (or trespasses / sins; cf. Luke 11:4), that is not the first to take place. First to take place is our forgiveness of others. The Greek tense make this clear: first aorist indcative is past tense: "we have forgiven."

---

[1]. Preached in the Covenant Church of Menominee, MI, on February 14, 1993.

"Forgive Us Our Debts"

The Bible in numerous places emphasizes the need for action on our part to occur before we request God's grace—which is what forgiveness is. John the Baptist says to the Pharisees and Sadducees: "You brood of vipers! Who warned you to flee from the wrath to come? Bear fruit worthy of repentance" (Matt 3:7–8). And in the Sermon on the Mount Jesus tells one bringing their gift to the altar to *first* seek the forgiveness of one they have wronged; then bring the offering (Matt 5:23–24). Paul warns us not to come to the communion table without first examining ourselves; otherwise we drink judgment on ourselves. He continues, "For this reason many of you are weak and ill, and some have died" (1 Cor 11:28–30).

All are warnings to those who have a "soft-soap" approach to God's grace, thinking God is flattered to be accessible anytime we call. All we have to do is come with our pleadings, regardless of the mess we have left outside our door or people we have trampled upon, and he will give us his loving attention. Not so. First we clean up the mess or amend the broken relationship; then we come to him. Action first; prayer to God second!

Having said this, we must not jump to the conclusion that this sequence of things is the only correct one. It is not. There are times when God deals with us before we get around to dealing with other people. There was Zacchaeus (Luke 19:1–10). Though the Bible says nothing about Zacchaeus seeking forgiveness from Jesus or Jesus giving it, it is sure to have happened. And when it did happen, we see this fellow going out straightaway to right the wrongs done to others. In Jesus' parable of the Unmerciful Servant, the king forgave the servant first; then the servant was expected to forgive the debt of someone else. He didn't, of course, but was expected to do so. The king representing God expects nothing less: that we forgive others after he has forgiven us.

We must, then, keep this petition of the Lord's Prayer together. Forgiveness from God goes hand in hand with forgiveness we grant others. If God acts first, we must act in kind. If God has not acted, very likely there is something we should be doing first before we come to him.

I'd like to say just a word also about this business of being in debt to God. We know what debts are, yet we cannot fully appreciate the seriousness of debt in antiquity when we can take out insurance, when we can file for bankruptcy, when limits exist on interest charges, and when slavery has been outlawed.

In ancient times you were sold into slavery if you couldn't pay your debts. Your family could also be sold. The servant in Jesus' parable is about to be sold with his family into slavery. The widow to whom Elisha came in 2 Kgs 4:1 faces the same horror—a creditor coming to take her two children to be slaves.

A person could be in debt through no fault of their own, e.g., sickness, bad crops, robbery victim, death of a spouse, etc. Or their indebtedness could be very much their own fault for the same reasons as today, e.g., foolish borrowing, foolish spending, or dishonesty. That perhaps explains why Matthew's version of the Prayer uses "debts" throughout. In Luke it is "forgive us our sins" (Luke 11:4), the older word being "trespasses." Debt is the broader term: It may include sin, it may not. In the OT Israel was in slavery not because of any sin, and God redeemed her. In the NT God has redeemed all people by the death of Jesus on the cross, and it was because they are sinners.

The New Testament message is that we are all debtors before God. The Pharisees had the idea—just as many modern people do—that good deeds could make up for bad deeds. But that isn't so, at least not in the economy of God.

Jesus purposely cites a huge sum of money in this parable (10,000 talents) to emphasize the impossibility of it being paid back. This is the state we are in before God. Our indebtedness is more than we can ever repay. We must therefore pray, "Forgive us our debts." The more difficult thing for us, no doubt, is to forgive one another, whether of debt or of wrongdoing. There are a number of pitfalls here, and I will touch on just a few this morning.

Sometimes we hesitate to forgive a person because it seems that if we do we are letting them off the hook. Perhaps if we didn't forgive them, they might not get away with what they did. Bad logic; bad psychology; bad theology.

"Forgive Us Our Debts"

When we forgive a person we are not letting them off the hook. We acknowledge their debt or wrong they committed. What is more, by forgiving we are dealing with it. Not forgiving someone is not to admit their debt or wrongdoing. It is also not dealing with it. which has more serious consequences.

If you do not forgive someone, chances are you will be the one who will pay. You may think the other person will be forced to pay, but it works in the reverse. People unable to forgive are some of the unhappiest people you will ever meet. The reason: Their unforgiving spirit is eating them out from inside.

Second, when we do forgive people, we wonder why it does not always make things the same as before. Sometimes, of course, it does, and sometimes things become better than before. But it nevertheless happens that vestiges of indebtedness and wrongdoing can remain. Why?

Probably because even though forgiveness has been granted and received, it is not as if the deed were never done. People who speak recklessly find this out. Words cannot be recalled once they are spoken, and remembrances of hurtful words remain, however much we wish otherwise. Husbands and wives who have been unfaithful learn this to their sorrow. Forgiveness can be given and accepted, but the deed can never be undone and never be completely forgotten, however much we wish otherwise. Forgiveness is a powerful force, but traces of the hurt may still remain, and we need to recognize this.

Third, forgiveness should mean that one is committed not to do again whatever it was they did. If for some individuals forgiveness is too hard a thing to do, for others it is too easy. They make a practice of doing wrong and then saying they are sorry. King Zedekiah thought he could release slaves one minute and take them back the next. He was commended for the debt he commuted, but Jeremiah and the Lord took an entirely different look at their action when he took back the slaves (Jer 34:8–22).

Jesus when he spoke to the woman caught in adultery said he did not condemn her, which could mean that he forgave her. But note what he adds, "Go, and don't do it again." Those words are just as important as forgiveness. When we forgive or when others forgive us it should be understood that we or they will not do wrong again. The unmerciful servant was forgiven when he fell to his knees, but he should not have gone out and acted badly again. In this case no mercy remained for the poor fellow.

Finally, the most remarkable teaching Jesus gives us about forgiveness is that we can forgive people in anticipation of their seeking it. We do not have to wait until they come and say "I'm sorry," even though that is what they should do and that is what they must do if forgiveness to take its full effect. When we discover anticipatory forgiveness we are in possession of one of the greatest powers contained in the Christian gospel. Jesus' words on the cross to those who put him there are the best example of forgiving before the fact. Paul too recognized this great truth, saying: "But God shows his love for us in that while we were yet sinners Christ died for us" (Rom 5:8).

Reconciliation is often long in coming. In fact, sometimes it never comes. Yet we can still forgive. It will free up our own selves. There is no reason for Christian people saying, "I can never forgive that person for what they did," even though John's Gospel does say: "if you retain the sins of any, they are retained" (John 20:23). God has forgiven us debts and sins we can never repay. We, likewise, can forgive the same others cannot repay.

The ways of sin are many. But the ways to God's grace are more. Have you received God's forgiveness, making you free to forgive others? Or are you holding forgiveness back, allowing your own soul to be eaten up while at the same time being cut off from God? Do you know we are all debtors before God and need a Savior? One has come. We call him Jesus. AMEN

11

"Deliver Us From Evil"[1]

Text: Matthew 6:13

And lead us not into temptation, but deliver us from evil

THE LAST PETITION OF the Lord's Prayer looks to the future. We are to pray: "And lead us not into temptation, but deliver us from evil / the Evil One." The NRSV reads: "And do not bring us to the time of trial, but rescue us from the evil one." The petition is difficult, which explains the different readings. Some ancient manuscripts of the Bible read "evil"; others "the evil one." The meaning, however, is not in doubt. We are asking God to deliver us from the power of evil.

The more difficult words are the prior ones: "and lead us not into temptation." Because lines in the petition are parallel we may think "temptation" is equivalent to "evil," but it is not. God does not lead us into evil! Greek πειρασμόν is broader and can mean "trial" or "testing" (NRSV). Perhaps then we are asking God not to lead us into a trial or a testing. Even when being tempted we know we are not fully in the territory of evil, although we are close.

---

1. Preached in the Covenant Church of Menominee, MI, on February 21, 1993.

I would call it being "close to the border," the border between right and wrong, good and evil, sometimes life and death. To be tempted or tested is not in itself bad. But you are never safe when it occurs. You are always at risk—at risk that you may fall.

This raises another problem. We do not like to think of God as one who tempts or tests. Yet in the Old Testament it happens: "After these things God tested Abraham" (Gen 22:1). We hear then how Abraham was asked by God to sacrifice his son Isaac. Abraham, of course, passed the test, and received God's favor. God also tested Moses when proposing to destroy a disobedent people and start all over again with him in building a nation (Exod 32:10). But Moses reminds God of his covenant with Abraham, and God turned back from the evil he had planned.

Another possibe interpretation of this difficult petition is that it makes use of an idiom called the "exaggerated contrast," where a statement is made simply to set off a second, which is the point being stressed. In this idiom the first of two statements cannot stand alone. In the NT, John says, "God did not send the Son into the world to condemn the world, but in order that the world might be saved through him" (John 3:17). Did Jesus' coming into the world condemn the world? Of course it did. But that was not God's purpose in sending Jesus. His reason was to save the world. The first statement simply sets off and heighten the importance of the second. The same could be happening here, because God does test and even tempt people, but our prayer is that God will deliver us from evil. That God will do.

The NT has a slightly different way of looking at matter. There God may lead a person to the place where he or she will be tested, or tempted, but does not do the actual tempting or testing. Not every NT writer states it as baldly as James who says that "[God] tempts no one" (Jas 1:13); the NT more often assumes that the tempting is done by Satan. When Jesus is 40 days in the wilderness Matthew says, "Then Jesus was led up by the Spirit into the wilderness to be tempted by the devil" (Matt 4:1). The Spirit, i.e., God, does the leading, but Satan does the tempting. Does God lead Jesus into temptation? Perhaps he does.

"Deliver Us From Evil"

We are still to pray, "Lead us not into temptation / trial." What can this mean? The NT is literally filled with passages telling us how Christians must undergo trials (and same Greek word πειρασμός is used):

> In this you rejoice, even if now for a little while you have had to suffer various *trials*, so that the genuineness of your faith—being more precious than gold, that, though perishable is tested by fire—may be found to result in praise and glory and honor when Jesus Christ is revealed (1 Peter 1:6–7)

> My brothers and sisters, whenever you face *trials* of any kind, consider it nothing but joy, because you know that the testing of your faith produces endurance ... Blessed is anyone who endures *temptation*. Such a one has stood the test and will receive the crown of life that the Lord has promised to those who love him (James 1:2–3, 12)

We get the impression from these passages that testing is a kind of muscle-building exercise that makes for strength and character—provided, of course, that one successfully passes the test. Wouldn't it be better to pray: "Lead us into temptation, Lord, for when we pass through the fiery furnace we will be stronger for it and more powerful in our witness, better prepared ..." or "Give us strength when temptations come—for you know that they are coming all the time—and help us overcome each one so we may go from one degree of glory to another ..."

What is the tone? Is it not overconfidence, which may give us a clue to what Jesus is asking for in the prayer he is teaching us. He may aim these words at our tendency to be overconfident about trials through which we have passed. I'm thinking of the Mission of the 70, who when they returned said, "I saw Satan fall like lightning out of heaven" (Luke 10:18). What does Jesus say to them? He sobers them up with a warning about being overconfident in God's power. He says, "Do not rejoice at this, that the spirits submit to you, but rejoice that your names are written in heaven" (Luke 10:20).

Paul has this very thing in mind in his word to the church at Corinth:

> So if you think you are standing, watch out that you do not fall. No testing has overtaken you that is not common to everyone. God is faithful, and he will not let you be tested beyond your strength, but with the testing he will also provide the way out so that you may be able to endure it. (1 Cor 10:12–13)

These words give us the confidence we need and ought to possess—that we can endure temptations and can trust God for help in overcoming them. We get a warning about thinking we are strong, which is the point at which we are in danger. Paul has just finished reminding his listeners about the generation in the wilderness—all of whom shared God's great act of salvation, and most of whom were tested and fell.

There are people today—maybe you are one of them—who can be cavalier about temptation. We say they like to "play with fire." They enjoy taking risks. They are the Evil Canevils, who head into danger like horses plunging headlong into battle (cf. Jer 8:6). People more sober know how close they are to the border when testing comes, how close they are to danger, how close they are to evil, how weak and vunerable they are, and had there been another combination of circumstances they might have fallen.

When you have been at the place where you have been severely tested and tried, you do not want to be there again. I do not believe for a moment that Abraham would want to go through his trial again, or that he would want anyone else to go through it. He would have willingly prayed Jesus' prayer. I do not believe Job would wish his testing on anyone. He too would have gladly prayed, "Lead me not into temptation." I do not believe any person in their right mind—who has gone through a fiery ordeal—wishes it to happen again. For such a person the words of this petition makes a lot of sense.

You know what I am talking about if you have gone through a difficult personal or family crisis; if you have been tempted to deceive parents or children; if you have fought off sexual urges at a

"Deliver Us From Evil"

time when the issue of right and wrong was before you but fading fast; if you had come close to giving full vent to your anger, or revenging a wrong committed you.

Some think Jesus may have had in mind the great period of trial said to accompany the End Times, the one he talks about in Matthew 24 where the scene is war with people fleeing cities and homes without having time to take extra clothing. He may have. If so, it makes good sense to pray "Lead us not into temptation / trial." Every now and then I encounter someone who is all excited about the End Times. They have been reading books and listening to impassioned preachers and say, "Isn't it exciting to be living in these days?" Let me tell you something. The trials of the End Times will be dreadful. No one—I mean no one—will be walking the streets saying, "Isn't it wonderful to be living in these days?"

No trial of God—especially the greatest trial for all humankind--gives one cause for buoyant optimism. It will be a time when people will be on the border for days, maybe weeks, and it will seem like forever; it will be a time when seemingly good people will do hideous things; it will be a time when some will live and some will die, some will be glorified and others will slip and fall.

The only thing one will be able to do is pray—pray that God will shorten the time, that he or she will not be led into testing but out of it, so they and everyone with them will not go under (Matt 24:22). That is what the End Times will be like. Jesus says pray that it will not come in winter (Matt 24:20). It is to humble us that Jesus has us pray, "And lead us not into temptation, and deliver us from evil / Evil One." We need help not to be led into dangerous situations. And we need help if we are going to be delivered from evil.

Finally, I believe God wants all of us to be his messengers in leading others away from temptation, and delivering others from evil. This work—like every other work of God—gets done through us. We must stay close to people who are going through trials, and give them the support that will keep them from danger, perhaps disaster. It may make the difference between them passing or not passing successfully through their trial. We may be the only ones who can help deliver friends and other folk from evil or the evil one. AMEN

Lent

12

"The Whole of Creation Waits"[1]

Text: Romans 8:22–23

We know that the whole creation has been groaning in labor pains until now; and not only the creation, but we ourselves, who have the first fruits of the Spirit, groan inwardly while we wait for adoption, the redemption of our bodies

IN 1923 ROBERT FROST wrote his poem "Fire and Ice." In it he said:

> Some say the world will end in fire
> Some say in ice
> From what I've tasted of desire
> I hold with those who favor fire
> But if it had to perish twice
> I think I know enough of hate
> To say that for destruction ice
> Is also great
> And would suffice.[2]

Astrophysicists today say that when the final solar convulsions take place, it will be first fire, then ice. The sun currently is

---

1. Preached in the Covenant Church of Menominee, MI, on March 21, 1993.

2. *Time* (March 23, 1987), 65.

in middle age: 4.5 billion years old, with some 5 billion years of life left. When the sun reaches the 10 billion year mark, and its fuel begins to run out, the nuclear fire will die down, the hydrogen fuel at the core will turn into helium, and it will begin to contract. Contraction at the core will force a rise in temperature, making the core of the sun hotter than ever.

Surface layers will cool and redden, making the sun a veritable red giant, increasing in size so as to encompass Mercury. Heat from the sun will be 500 to 1000 times as great as today; oceans will boil and life will be incinerated. Eventually, after cycles of contraction and re-expansion, the sun will become a lump no bigger than earth. Its nuclear fires will no longer burn, and it will cool slowly and end up a cold black cinder. Lifeless earth will then pass into an eternal deep-freeze. First fire, then ice.

A few years ago we heard about an exploding star, or "supernova." One had not been visible to the naked eye since 1885, but in February 1987 a supernova was observed by a Canadian astronomer in an observatory in northern Chile. This latest explosion took place 170,000 years ago, when early intelligent Homo sapiens on the earth were fashioning crude axes out of stone. Only now had the light reached the earth.

These explosions are but a stage in the death of a star in some far-off galaxy, a spectacular display of what for our sun is still a prediction. It is a sign, all the same, that our earth is groaning in travail-like rhythms towards an eventual death. Some anthropologists predict that human life as we know it will be extinct on our planet in 400 years—due to the lack of a food supply and other life-preserving forces.

If you have visited someone recently who is in their advanced years, you will hear them tell you that their body is wearing out. My grandfather's sister used to say, "My right leg says yes, and my left leg says no." Someone you know with an advanced illness may be in a worse condition, where the groanings for redemption are a veiled call for death.

Paul, in our text and in the lesson from Romans 8 is aware that he and the rest of creation are subjected by God to futility, are in bondage to decay, are groaning together in travail. Like others in antiquity he had a more unified view of the created order than we have today. People then, and to some extent people up to the 16th c. when the Copernican revolution took place, had the notion that what happened in the heavens affected what happened on earth, what happened in the lives of the king, his subjects—and the animals too—was one orchestrated activity of the creation.

Thus it was in Babylon, almost 5000 years ago, that astrology developed. Astrologers believed that the fate of human beings could be discerned, yes, even controlled by the sun, moon, and the planets. Planets were identified with the Babylonian gods, e.g., Jupiter was Marduk and Venus was Ishtar. It was also believed that even little things in individual lives, such as happiness (not little, really) and bad fortune (also not little) depended upon phenomena in the heavens.

Today, over 300 years after the earth was identified as one of the heavenly bodies, and astronomy was finally rid of ancient astrological notions, we still find people returning to these ancient ideas. They read horoscopes and to some extent believe them: they believe depression has to do with dreary weather in March, being pent up in the house, etc. A lady in the Post Office the other day was talking about her recent trip to Las Vegas, and how she played the slots a certain way because it was her birthday. The cult leader, David Koresh, in Waco, TX, is curretly waiting for some astrological sign before making his next move.

The Bible, despite its age, long ago parted company with astrological notions, mainly because it believed in one God who created and controlled one universe. But Jewish people and also early Christians believed nevertheless that the created order possessed an essential unity, and that stars and barking dogs could give witness to acts of God just as much as men and women.

When the people of Israel left Egypt Moses said that while the cry of the Egyptians who had lost their first-borns would be ever so great (like the mothers of Bosnia who have lost their children), not a dog would growl against them as they prepared to depart (Exod 11:7). Here creation was joining in at the redemption of Israel.

You Are the Light of the World

The year was 1692. The place: Salem, Massachusetts in Puritan New England. The date was September 22, when seven witches and one lone wizard were packed into a cart and hauled the long mile to Gallows Hill. The sheriff had chosen the most conspicuous spot for the hangings, even if it was not the most convenient. Rev. Nicholas Noyes, senior pastor of the First Church in Salem Town, referred to them on that day as the "eight firebrands of hell." Some were fiery. But there was Mary Esty, who in her last appeal spoke not of her own innocence—which she had always maintained—but of the innocence of others and the need to show mercy towards them. There was Martha Cory, an honest woman with unquestioned integrity in the community, who, ascended the ladder with a prayer on her lips. We are told that as each one took their last look over the distant waters of Massachusetts Bay, the sky was gray and overcast, with rain threatening. The whole of creation was mourning, and set to weep

The year was 1964. The place Beirut, Lebanon. We were gathered, members of the American Community Church at the University Christian Center in West Beirut to hear a debate over a new book published by Paul VanBuren. One of the debaters, Hugh Harcourt, taught philosophy at the American University of Beirut, and was a respected member of the church. The other was also faculty at the University, but a professed atheist.

As the atheist began to speak we could hear the rain beating on the roof. Then he came to a point, where, out of his mouth came the words, "I do not believe in God." At that moment a terrific bolt of thunder struck. The timing was so exact that everyone spontaneously broke out in laughter.

Afterwards my professor of Old Testament at the Near East School of Theology commented that had such a thing happened in ancient Israel everyone would have spontaneously fallen down on their knees. They would have recognized that creation was protesting loudly at the outrage.

The date was February 19, 1980. We had gathered out at the North Hilmar (CA) Cemetery to lay the body of a boy not yet 2 years old into the ground. It had been raining hard all morning.

"The Whole of Creation Waits"

Now, only minutes before the service, it stopped. At the close of the service, just as I began reading words from Scripture about the resurrection of Jesus and the Christian hope, the sun came out briefly to warm us; in a moment it was gone. Everyone took notice. The creation had been weeping even as we were weeping. Then for one brief moment it smiled, telling us that it too was waiting with eager longing for the revealing of one of the sons of God.

Three of the gospel writers, Matthew, Mark and Luke, record what must have been a widespread observation, that at the time of Jesus' crucifixion there was darkness over the whole land. It lasted from the sixth hour to the ninth hour (which is from noon to three in the afternoon—usually the brightest hours of the day (cf. Mark 15:33). The creation was mourning the death of Jesus. The curtain of the temple was rent from top to bottom, which Matthew attributes to a violent trembling of the earth that left rocks split and tombs opened (Matt 27:51–52).

The violent trembling of creation was noted by none other than a Gentile, a Roman centurion standing by the cross. He remarked, "Truly this man was God's son" (Mark 15:39). The first of God's sons—and daughters—was revealed. And it did not go unnoticed how the creation brightened up at Jesus' resurrection. In Luke 24:4 we are told that angels at the tomb were standing in "dazzling apparel." What does this mean if not that the sun was shining brightly on their clothes, a sure sign that the creation was no longer in bondage to decay, was greeting with joy its glorious redemption, and had seen the first of God's sons—the one Jesus Christ—revealed.

For Paul Jesus' suffering and death profoundly affected the creation—indeed it was part of and in rhythm with that mighty act of God whose purpose was to redeem everything. But the rest of creation, he observed, was still groaning—like a woman in travail. It was in bondage to decay; it awaited its glorious redemption; it longed eagerly to see the sons of God revealed.

Today creation continues to wait with eager longing for the revealing of God's sons and daughters. Thank God for redemption in Christ Jesus. Is that redemption an assured reality for you? AMEN

Holy Week

13

"It Is Expedient That One Man Should Die"[1]

Text: John 11:49-50

But one of them, Caiaphas, who was high priest that year, said to them, "You know nothing at all! You do not understand that it is better for you to have one man die for the people than to have the whole nation destroyed"

EVERY TIME I READ Gospel accounts of the Passion I am overwhelmed at the enormity of evil shown in the face of good, the enormity of blindness on the part of people who took part in the drama, and the enormity of God's power—that all this evil, all this confusion, all this blindness could work together to bring God's purpose about, and could work for our ultimate good.

Something similar happened in ancient Greek drama. In the end, when the plot got so involved, so confused, and so incapable of resolution, a *deus ex machina* had to be brought in, i.e., a god on some sort of machine, and this god straightened things out. No one else could.

---

1. Preached in the Covenant Church of Menominee, MI, on March 28, 1993.

You Are the Light of the World

We see confusion and fear in the Pharisees and Sadducees (chief priests), who did not know what to do with Jesus because he had performed many mighty works. He had just raised Lazarus. They envision the whole nation going after Jesus, which, they said, will bring the Romans in to destroy the Jewish people and their temple. The high priest, Caiaphas, said others didn't know what they were talking about. He did, however, say "it is expedient that one man should die for the people." But the Gospel writer says the high priest did not know what he was saying, even though his words would turn out to be prophetic beyond anyone's imagination.

We might expect Pilate, who was Roman, to be clueless when it came to understanding Jesus, for he knew nothing about salvation history at the heart of Jewish faith. Pilate comes off, quite expectedly, as one who would just as soon have had nothing to do with Jesus and the internal dissension he was causing among Jews. Mark says Pilate "was amazed" after interrogating Jesus (Mark 15:5). He publicly washed his hands of Jesus' blood (Matt 27:24). And his most famous statement of all at the trial was when he said, "What is truth?" (John 18:38).

Caiaphas, however, was "an insider," the high priest who, according to Jewish law, was without sin and by his own admission one possessing knowledge others did not possess. Let us look for a few moments at Caiaphas. The situation required that he become involved. The raising of Lazarus had caused a great stir. Some who had witnessed it went and told the Pharisees. Whether these were believers in Jesus, friends of the Pharisees, or just tale-bearers, we do not know. They may have included all three. The Sanhedrin was called into session. It was the highest Jewish council made up of Sadducees and Pharisees. These groups were usually at odds with one another—kind of like Democrats and Republicans in the US Congress—but on this occasion they looked at each other and said, "What shall we do?" It was conceded that Jesus had performed many miracles, but this could not go on, so the argument ran, lest the Romans interpret his messiahship as a direct threat to their rule and come to destroy Jerusalem, the temple, and the Jewish nation (John 11:48).

"It Is Expedient That One Man Should Die"

Something similar—although not quite the same—is going on today in Russia. The congress, made up of old Communists for the most part, is fearful of a President who wants to change things and who also enjoys wide public support. They want to impeach him. Now, however, because they do not have the votes, they are talking about "other options."

Caiaphas is not talking release. It is Passover, sacrifice time, and he is thinking "death." For him it is a political move, but also a judgment made on religious and theological grounds. Caiaphas is today what we would call a "political person." We know this by his use of the word "expedient." He says it is expedient that one person should die so the whole nation might live. Expedient means "profitable, useful, for the sake of unity." Can one argue against the idea that the common good must be served?

In antiquity when a war was being fought and you were unable to hold out any longer, you would surrender to the enemy the person most responsible for resistance. This would pacify the enemy, and the war would end. In 2 Sam 20:14–22 Joab, David's general, besieged Bethmaacah because Sheba, who was threatening David's rule, had found refuge there. In this city was not a wise high priest, but rather a wise woman who advised that the head of Sheba be thrown over the city wall to Joab. The whole city might then be spared. People of the city listened. Sheba's head was cut off, and thrown over the city wall. The war was over; the trumpet was blown, and everyone went home. It was expedient that one man die for the people.

Caiaphas is offering similar counsel. The city was afraid of being besieged by the legions of Rome, and must therefore give up the person responsible for the insurrection before all go under. Was it a groundless fear? Maybe. Maybe not. As high priest, Caiaphas perhaps had another fear, this one having to do not with Rome but with God. He sees in the increasing popularity of Jesus—now especially after the raising of Lazarus—that the entire religious establishment in Jerusalem be in danger of crumbling. If so, it could be a sign of God's anger, and that anger must be appeased. How does one appease God's anger? A priest should know.

One offers up a sacrifice! In ancient times you appeased an angry god by making a sacrifice. The King of Moab, when the battle was going against him, offered up his eldest son as a burnt offering. It turned the tide of the battle, and the enemy withdrew (2 Kgs 3:27). Chemosh, god of the Moabites was appeased.

Something similar happened in Israel: The person or persons thought to be responsible for God's anger had to be sacrificed, i.e., killed, to save the nation. When the people of Israel began to flirt with Baal of Peor in the wilderness, the Lord became angry. Moses was therefore commanded by the Lord to hang the chiefs responsible in the sun so his anger would be appeased. A plague nevertheless followed, and it was a priest, Phinehas, who put the sword to an Israelite man and his Midianite girlfriend, stopping the plague. For this act of valor Phinehas was given the Lord's "covenant of peace" (Num 25:1–15). Compare what happened when a man named Achan took some of the spoils after the defeat of Jericho—a beautiful coat, 200 sheckles of silver, and a bar of gold weighing 50 sheckles. This so angered the Lord that Joshua and his army were defeated by an inferior army from Ai. Here lots had to be drawn to find the culprit, and after Achan was discovered and he confessed, they stoned him; his family and everything he had—including his animals—were burned. This turned the Lord from his burning anger (Joshua 7).

In viewing Jesus as an enemy of the high priest we may forget that Jesus was nevertheless considered to be one of them, i.e., the one making God angry against the Jewish people. In some ancient biblical manuscripts v 50 reads, "... it is expedient *for us* that one man should die ..." There is no doubt that the high priest thought of himself—and colleagues who voted for Jesus' death—as being with God on the right side, and Jesus being on the wrong side. At the same time, Caiaphas may have been conceding that the Jewish nation was guilty. In any case, Jesus had to be sacrificed in order to preserve the nation. So Caiaphas led the move to arrest Jesus and see that he was put to death. But in reading John's gospel we see that Caiaphas was still "in the dark." He says more than he

"It Is Expedient That One Man Should Die"

knows, for his decision will indeed save the Jewish people in a way he knows not. More than that, it will save the world!

It was not God's anger that needed appeasement, as the Swedish theologian P. P. Waldenström argued many years ago. It was God's love showing through an incomprehensible web of human fear, hatred, foolishness, and confusion. John 3:16 is a commentary on all this: "For God so *loved* the world . . ."

Another passage of Scripture is also suitable comment for what was taking place during these fateful days in Jerusalem. It is found in Micah 6:6–8. What does the Lord require when we seek him in a moment of great vexation and trouble, even sin? Does he want sacrifices, the first-borns of our bodies? No, the Lord does not want this. What the Lord requires is that we do justice, love the covenant / kindness, and walk humbly with our God.

Caiaphas did none of these. He knew nothing about justice. Jesus did no wrong like Israel did in the wilderness, or like Achan did. True wisdom always requires one to act on more than political expediency, to understand right from wrong, miracle from fraud, innocence from guilt. Caiaphas did not love the covenant, for the covenant would never have given him the right to plot the death of a righteous Jew. Worst of all, Caiaphas was not humble before God. He didn't even talk about God. The gospel record makes this transparent. He claims to know when he does not know. And he ends up—despite being a prophet—in the dark, because his deeds were evil.

The Pharisee Gamaliel, who was a teacher of the Apostle Paul, was wiser and more humble when he advised the same Jewish Sanhedrin in how to deal with Peter and the disciples. They wanted to kill them, but Gamaliel said these remarkable words:

> So in the present case I tell you, keep away from these men and let them alone; because if this plan or this undertaking is of human origin, it will fail; but if it is of God, you will not be able to overthrow them—in that case you may even be found fighting against God (Acts 5:38–39)

You Are the Light of the World

As we continue in our Lenten reflection this morning, let us test our thoughts, our wisdom, our doings, and all feelings of anxiety, bitterness, and judgment over against Jesus and the cross. We may know less than we think. We may say things, which, to our embarassment, will be turned by God into something other than what we intended. We may be blinded by ideas about numbers and what we think it takes to bring unity. We may be unwilling to acknowledge that God is doing miracles we are not a part of. We may be jealous because belief is coming to others in different ways than it came to us. In our perplexing times may we rather focus on what God really requires, that we do justice, love the covenant, and walk humbly with our God. AMEN.

14

"Father Forgive Them, for They Know Not What They Do"[1]

Text: Luke 23:34

Then Jesus said, "Father, forgive them; for they do not know what they are doing." And they cast lots to divide his clothing

ALL FOUR NEW TESTAMENT Gospels contain words Jesus spoke from the cross. They are seven in number, now immortalized by Théodore DuBois' "Seven Last Words of Christ" (1807). The first word has to do with forgiveness: "Father, forgive them; for they do not know what they are doing." When we hear these words, which are spoken to God but directed as much to Jesus' enemies, we are prone to say, "My what grace, what love beyond measure!" How can Jesus, in a moment of great agony forgive those who condemned him to die?

Yes, there is love beyond measure, and grace too. But this is not what Jesus' enemies will hear if any are standing at the foot of the cross. They will hear something quite different. For the high priest, the pompous Pharisee, the rich lawyer—indeed anyone

---

1. Lenten Meditation at the Covenant Church of Menominee, MI, on February 24, 1993.

who said "yes" to what was taking place, these words will come as a rebuke. According to Rabbinic law a condemned criminal, before his execution, was supposed to say these words: "May my death expiate all *my* sins."[2] Death atones for sin, and when a guilty person dies, he dies for his own sins. If that person can be moved to contrition, he will say, "Father, forgive me, for I did not know what I was doing."

This is what those two young boys from Liverpool should be praying today; what the leaders of Serbia should be praying; what anyone should be praying when brought to justice for crimes outraging human sensibility. It is what anyone should say for committing lesser wrongs.

But Jesus says, "Father forgive them . . ." What we are listening to are the words of an innocent man, one who knows he is innocent, one who must put the blame, the guilt, the burden of asking for forgiveness where it belongs—squarely on those who put him where he is. Will his enemies be perceptive enough to hear it? Probably, and if so, they will know they have been rebuked with the words. Jesus is not dying for his own sins; he is dying for the sins of the world.

Love and grace will be felt later—when enemies and anyone else who consented to his death come under conviction, when they realize that they really did not know what they were doing, and ask to be forgiven. The emphasis then will not be on "them," which was so piercing at first, but on "forgive." This double-edged remark will now have new meaning. Jesus will be seen as a forgiving friend, one pleading to God on their behalf.

Do not think that all sins are intentional, premeditated, naked acts of wrongdoing. Some are, but more, I think, are done without one knowing what he or she is doing. Satan is not a transparent outlaw; he is an outlaw masquerading as an angel of light.

The Roman centerion was the first to recognize what was going on. We are told that while everyone else was going home beating their breasts, this man praised God when Jesus breathed

---

2. J. Jeremias, *The Central Message of the New Testament* (Minneapolis: Fortress, 1981), 48.

"Father Forgive Them, for They Know Not What They Do"

his last, saying, "Certainly, this man was innocent" (Luke 23:47). "The sons of this world are wiser in their own generation than the sons of light" (Luke 16:8).

And what about those 3000 people at Pentecost who came under conviction, and repented? Had Jesus gone from being an enemy to being a friend? Has it happened to you? Are you reconciled to God? Is Jesus no longer your enemy but a friend? Either way, this prayer is for you, for me, for everyone in whatever state we find ourselves: "Father, forgive them, for they do not know what they are doing." AMEN

15

"Today You Will Be With Me in Paradise"[1]

Text: Luke 23:42–43

Then he said, "Jesus, remember me when you come into your kingdom." He replied, "Truly I tell you, today you will be with me in Paradise."

THIS WORD FROM THE cross culminates a brief exchange that took place between Jesus and two criminals who were crucified with him. Jesus had already spoken a word of forgiveness to others—rulers, perhaps, and others who were scoffing at him. The one criminal had joined in the mocking, saying, "Are you not the Christ? Save yourself and us!"

Now the other criminal speaks up, and is lucid enough to say to the other thief: "Do you not fear God? You, too, my friend, are under condemnation of death. What is more, we are getting our due. But this man has done nothing wrong." We may think it remarkable to hear a criminal speak the truth, but criminals can and do speak the truth.

---

1. Meditation at a joint Lenten service held at the Trinity Episcopal Church, Thomaston, CT, on April 1, 1988.

"Today You Will Be With Me in Paradise"

His anger is our anger, an anger welling up whenever we encounter people who are "puffed up" and unrepentant of evil they have done. A recurring phenomenon among the unrepentant is that they exaggerate their innocence and play down or deny their guilt. Sin is consistently underestimated, said to be not very bad, not bad at all, or perhaps even justifiable if only we knew "where they were coming from."

This brief exchange taking place between one criminal and Jesus is a remarkable one. After the man has rebuked his fellow criminal, he says: "Jesus, remember me when you come into your kingdom." The words are rightly taken to be words of contrition and faith. They presuppose repentance, which, if not spoken to the rabbi before being nailed to the cross as Jewish custom required, were spoken now. He said, "we are getting what we deserve for our deeds."

The request made to Jesus is a modest one, "Remember me." The man is not presumptuous enough to think he will have any place in the new kingdom, for he does not deserve one. He will take whatever he gets. The man is unable to pray to God directly. He needs a mediator, a go-between, and that one becomes Jesus. How often I have heard people who are themselves afraid to pray, say, "Pray for me." Jesus can remember the fellow before God. That will be enough.

It is what Joseph asked the chief butler to do when the two were together in prison, and the dream Joseph interpreted for him indicated that he would be restored three days hence. Joseph said, "But remember me when it is well with you; please do me the kindness to make mention of me to Pharaoh, and get me out of this place" (Gen 40:14). Because the request of this criminal on the cross is a modest one—and it is modest, since the man is guilty of a capital offense—Jesus speaks these remarkable words: "Truly I tell you, today you will be with me in Paradise." The great Saint Ambrose, Bishop of Milan (A.D. 374–397), correctly saw in these words an important element in divine grace. He said, "The Lord always grants more than the repentant asks for."

The man asks only to be remembered when Jesus gets into his kingdom, which will presumably be before he gets there, that is, if he does get there. From the Joseph story we recall it was to be "three days." But Jesus, dispensing God's grace and mercy, says, "Today you will be with me in Paradise." Ambros was right: the man got more than he asked for.

There was a "getting more than what was asked for" in Jesus' teachings and miracles. When Jesus was on his way to the home of Jairus to heal his daughter, word came while he was still on the road that the daughter was dead. But Jesus went anyway, and raised the twelve-year old after coming into the house (Luke 8:40–42, 49–56). Jesus fed a crowd of 5000 with bread and fish enough for perhaps five or six people (Luke 9:12–17). Jesus teaches that one should take the lowest seat at a wedding reception; then one might get invited to sit at a place much better (Luke 14:7–11). The lost son in Jesus' parable asks on his return home to be but a hired servant, but the father puts the best robe on him, places a ring on his hand, sandals on his feet, kills the fatted calf, and throws a party (Luke 15:11–32). And the servant in Jesus' parable who pleads for more time to pay his debt, has the entire debt forgiven on the spot (Matt 18:23–35).

We can learn three important lessons from this exchange on the cross: 1) about the proper posture of a sinner; 2) about the posture of God when a sinner repents; and 3) about the importance of faith. The proper posture of a sinner is to admit more and ask for less. The Lord, on his part, will grant more to the repentant sinner than what he asks for. As for the one who has faith, even an amount as small as a grain of mustard seed will move mountains (Matt 17:20). A veritable mountain stood before this criminal and the Kingdom of God. To one who has faith will more be given (Matt 13:12). To one without faith, what he does have, namely, delusions about self, others, and above all about God, will evaporate. AMEN

16

"Woman, Here Is Your Son ... Here Is Your Mother"[1]

Text: John 19:26–27

When Jesus saw his mother and the disciple whom he loved standing beside her, he said to his mother, "Woman, here is your son." Then he said to the disciple, "Here is your mother." And from that hour the disciple took her into his own home

THE SCENE DEPICTED BY the writer of the Fourth Gospel is humiliating and at the same time touching. Roman soldiers have stripped Jesus of his clothes before nailing him to the cross, and now they are dividing the garments among themselves. The only comparable custom I can think of, and it is a Jewish custom, is one where a wife being divorced is stripped of her clothes by her husband. He does this not only to humiliate her, but because the clothes are technically his.

Here at the cross women are present. If women today are indignant about unclothed women pictured in men's magazines, and some are, it is no less the case that men feel shame when another man's clothes are stripped off before women. Among the women

[1]. Meditation at joint Lenten service held at the Trinity Episcopal Church, Thomaston, CT, on April 20, 1984.

here at the cross is one to which we take particular notice. It is Mary, Jesus' mother. Since Jesus did not have a wife, the clothes he wore Mary probably made for him.

Mary was there when Jesus came naked into the world—that night in Bethlehem. Is she remembering that? Mary took particular delight in dressing her child. We know the Christmas story. "And (she) wrapped him in bands of cloth and laid him in a manger" (Luke 2:7). Now the process is reversed: her son's clothes are rudely taken off while she looks on. Jesus knows she is there. The text says he saw her standing next to the beloved disciple (v 26). Jesus speaks to her: "Woman, here is your son." Did she not know that? Did she not see what had taken place, and was she not standing there helpless at this final indignity? What was Mary doing if she was not looking at her son?

But again, as so often happens, Jesus' words have another meaning or perhaps double meaning. We do not perceive this until he speaks again, which he does after a moment of silence. Glancing now toward the beloved disciple, he says, "Here is your mother." It becomes clear. Jesus is not so much calling attention to himself, as we thought, or as Mary thought. He is directing attention to two important people standing at the foot of the cross: His mother and the beloved disciple. A new relationship is being formed; Mary is to look at the beloved disciple as her son; the beloved disciple is to behold Mary as his mother. The text goes on to say that from that hour the disciple took her into his own home. Tradition has it that the "beloved disciple" was John, and a Church of St. John (*Agios Theologos*) in Selçuk, Turkey, one mile from Ephesus, marks the place where John was buried and is said to have cared for Mary in his last days. Nearby is a House of the Virgin Mary about which the tradition is less certain. The church played an important role in Christian pilgrimages in the Middle Ages.

Jesus had spoken in a similar vein before. When his mother and brothers came one day and were tryng to speak to him, he said, "Who are my mother and my brothers? . . . Here are my mother and my brothers! Whoever does the will of God is my brother and sister and mother" (Mark 3:31–34). Shocking words. But are we

"Woman, Here Is Your Son... Here Is Your Mother"

not concerned today about the family? We should be; it is today being diminished or treated with disrespect by professionals and more ordinary people.

There is a teaching here, however, which is not anti-family, but which sees the Kingdom as the larger family of God. In this family our sons and daughters become sons and daughters of others, and we adopt moms and dads, also children of various ages, even though none are blood relatives. Linda and I have always encouraged our children to seek nurture from others besides ourselves, even though we try our best to be nurturant parents. Good families transcend themselves in the church, where they can become more than they are on their own.

Remember the story of Ruth and Naomi? Naomi and her husband left Bethlehem for Moab in order to escape a famine. In Moab Naomi lost her husband. Her two sons married Moabite women, and after ten years the sons died, leaving Naomi with her two Moabite daughters-in-law. When Naomi decided to return home, she urged the daughters-in-law to leave her and return to their mothers' house (Ruth 1:8). There they could get other husbands and establish a home. Naomi blessed them in the name of the Lord. Orpha decided to return home, but not Ruth. Her words to Naomi are familiar:

> Where you go, I will go
> Where you lodge, I will lodge
> Your people shall be my people
> and your God my God.
> Where you die, I will die—
> there will I be buried.
> (Ruth 1:16–17)

This moves us because Ruth treats Naomi as a mother, even though she is not really her mother. How many young boys and girls, men and women, need mothers today? And fathers? How many women and men have no children, but wish they did? Your mother can be the widow in your midst; it can be the mother who has lost her child; it can be any woman your senior to whom you might relate with love and affection. God's Kingdom is a family, in large measure because of Jesus' words from the cross: "Woman, here is your son . . . Here is your mother." AMEN

17

"My God, My God, Why Have You Forsaken Me?"[1]

Text: Mark 15:34; Matt 27:46

At three o'clock Jesus cried out in a loud voice, "Eloi, Eloi, lema sabachthani?" which means, "My God, my God, why have you forsaken me?"

I THINK OF ALL the words that Jesus spoke from the cross, these are the most difficult to hear—the anguished cry of one fully human who feels God had forsaken him. We don't hear the familiar "Father," spoken in the prayer for his enemies. How differently Jesus dies than the celebrated hero of Greek antiquity, Socrates. Socrates drinks the cup of death without a murmur, talking calmly with his disciples to the end. The only cries to be heard are those from his disciples, who cannot bear to see the life of this great man slowly ebb away. For the Greeks death was a friend; for the Hebrews it was an enemy—Paul says it is "the last enemy to be destroyed" (1 Cor 15:26).

I think, however, that what disturbs us most is the apparent lack of an answer to Jesus' cry. When Jesus was born angels from

1. Lenten Meditation at the Covenant Church of Hilmar, CA, on March 23, 1978.

heaven sang; when he was baptized by John the heavens opened, and a voice said, "You are my son, the Beloved; with you I am well pleased" (Mark 1:11). The same words were uttered from heaven when Jesus was transfigured on the mountain (Matt 17:5). But here there is silence. We know where Jesus' words come from. They begin Psalm 22:

> My God, my God, why have you forsaken me?
>   Why are you so far from helping me
>   from the words of my groaning?
>   (Psa 22:1)

But in the Psalm the opening words are answered:

> I will tell of thy name to my brethren
>   in the midst of the congregation I will praise thee
> You who fear the LORD, praise him!
>   all you sons of Jacob, glorify him
>   and stand in awe of him, all you sons of Israel!
> For he has not despised or abhorred
>   the affliction of the afflicted
> And he has not hid his face from him
>   but has heard, when he cried to him. . .
>   (Psa 22:22–24)

Jesus doubtless knew the entire psalm, and while it is too long for him to have recited it all in his suffering, he knew how it ended. His cry was answered.

There is another cry in the Old Testament similar to this one. It comes from the prophet Jeremiah. Fearing that he is about to meet death, he curses the day he was born and concludes his lament with these words:

> *Why did I come forth from the womb*
>   to see toil and sorrow
>   and end my days in shame?
>   (Jer 20:18 AB)

"My God, My God, Why Have You Forsaken Me?"

Here too is no reply, which led the great Old Testament scholar, Gerhard von Rad, to say, "the God whom the prophet addresses no longer answers him."[2]

Yet there was an answer. These desparate words were answered by the scribe compiling the book's First Edition with words Jeremiah heard at the time of his call, when God said:

> Before I formed you in the belly I knew you
> and *before you came forth from the womb* I consecrated you
> I appointed you a prophet to the nations
> (Jer 1:5 AB)

After the passing of time, a time of some waiting, an answer did come. God was not silent.

Nor was God silent here. In just three days God spoke loudly by raising Jesus from the dead. And the echo of that dramatic word has been heard for nearly 2000 years as the resurrection of Jesus has been proclaimed throughout the world in word, in song, and by men and women living and dying in Jesus' name. It was heard by the disciples on Easter. It was heard on Pentecost by Peter and a multitude. It has been heard by a mighty army down through the ages up to the present day. The answer is proclaimed here tonight, and it will be proclaimed with more joy on Easter Sunday. The proclamation will continue until Christ returns. AMEN

---

2. Gerhard von Rad, *Old Testament Theology II* (trans. D. M. G. Stalker; London: SCM Press, 1953), 204.

18

"I Am Thirsty"[1]

Text: John 19:28

After this, when Jesus knew that all was now finished, he said (in order to fulfill the scripture), "I am thirsty"

WHEN JESUS WAS BEING nailed to the cross, which must have been an unspeakably painful experience, he was offered a cup of wine mixed with gall. This small act of mercy would lessen his pain. But two Gospel writers tell us that he refused it (Mark 15:23, which has "mixed with myrrh"; Matt 27:34). Matthew says he tasted it, but would not drink it.

Now when he is on the cross, there are offers of ὄξος, "sour wine," or "vinegar," which is a cheap wine used by soldiers and laborers to quench their thirst. Luke says the soldiers offered it as a mocking gesture (Luke 23:36). Kind if like, "Want a drink, King of the Jews?" Maybe they themselves had a bit too much. Their job, after all, was not a pleasant one.

The offer comes also from bystanders who appear to be Jews. Both Mark and Matthew note that they offer Jesus sour wine after hearing him cry, "Eli, . . . Eli . . . " (Matt 27:48), misinterpreting the

---

1. Lenten Meditation given at the Covenant Church of Menominee, MI on March 24, 1993.

"I Am Thirsty"

words to be a call for Elijah. Even though they mishear, they are able to discern the Aramaic, which the Romans probably would have missed, for they knew Elijah, the great savior of Judaism. The wine was offered on a sponge, held up on a branch (of hyssop?). Neither Gospel writer says he took it.

There was confusion, to be sure, among the bystanders. According to Mark, the wine seems to be offered in the hopes that Jesus might be kept alive a moment longer, in which case Elijah could come to save him. But in Matthew's Gospel, those hoping for Elijah to come urge that he not be given the wine, at least not yet. They say, "Wait, let us see whether Elijah will come to save him." Here the idea is that the wine might hasten his death. But in both cases, the hope was that Jesus would be rescued. Elijah, however, did not come.

According to John, Jesus knew things were finished, for which reason he said, "I am thirsty." Here, when the wine on the sponge was offered, he accepted it; John is the only Gospel writer to tell us that. He said this was to fulfill Scripture. There are two possible Scriptures John may have had in mind. One was Psalm 22, part of which Jesus already uttered on the cross. In this psalm it says:

> I am poured out like water
>   and all my bones are out of joint
> My heart is like wax
>   it is melted within my breast
> My mouth is dried up like a potsherd
>   and my tongue sticks to my jaws
>   you lay me in the dust of death
>   (Psa 22:14–15)

The other psalm is Psalm 69, which says:

> They gave me poison for food
>   and for my thirst they gave me vinegar to drink
>   (Psa 69:21)

In the Septuagint, the same word, ὄξος, "sour wine" is used.

John gives a positive interpretation of this wine-drinking just before Jesus died. In his view, Jesus accepts death as God's suffering

Messiah. In his view, there is salvation even though Elijah did not come. Drinking the wine, even though it be cheap wine, and the mention of "hyssop," give us clear references to the Passover celebration. The hyssop was used to sprinkle the blood of the Passover lamb on the doorposts (Exod 12:22), and the wine, of course, was part of the Passover meal. It is ironic that Jesus was sentenced to death at the very hour when the slaughtering of the lambs began in the temple (John 19:14). Now Jesus, the Lamb of God, has been sacrificed for the sins of the world.

Are we not often like those standing at the foot of the cross, who see in tragedy and death around us the meaninglessness of it all, or perhaps the absence of salvation instead of God's hidden deliverance? We fumble around amidst those we love, wanting to give them something to drink, wondering if perhaps we should wait for the doctor, and so on. Even after our loved one has died, we wonder what might have happened if we had done things differently. We do these things, but we know it will not change what is taking place. For Christians, however, is a much greater message, which is that death is transformed into victory.

We also learn from this word on the cross that the simple request for a drink, even in the last moments of life, is to be honored. Jesus taught us earlier:

> Whoever gives you a cup of water to drink
> because you bear the name of Christ will by
> no means lose the reward (Mark 9:41). AMEN

19

"It Is Finished!"[1]

Text: John 19:30

When Jesus had received the wine, he said, "It is finished."
Then he bowed his head and gave up his spirit

IN HEBREW IT IS just one word: *kālāh*; in Arabic it would be *kalas*. The latter they say in Arab countries when you are finished with immigration at the border and they hand back your passport: *kalas*. If they use English, it is simply "finish." I wonder how it sounded when Jesus spoke it, the tone of his voice, whether he spoke it with strength, or whether there was a sigh accompanying it. Maybe the word was just a whisper. Still, I wonder how it sounded. This word from the cross is usually taken as Jesus' word of triumph, so maybe he spoke it in a loud voice. Was Jesus just glad to get the suffering over? I imagine so. We have heard people make similar utterances after finishing an unpleasant task. "It's finished" (sigh). "I am glad that's over." "Was than an ordeal!" These are all familiar responses, but with Jesus it is dying a painful death.

Others saying "It is finished" do so with hurt in their voice. I'm thinking of people for whom life has been hard, filled with

1. Meditation at a joint Lenten service held at Bethlehem Lutheran Church, Thomaston, CT, on April 17, 1987.

disappointment, not what they hoped for. People in all ages have been profoundly dissatisfied with life because of a disappointed love, unfulfilling work, or because they were victim of some personal or national tragedy—the Vietnam war, for example. Such people may even have what we call the "death wish."

The Greek poet Euripides in "The Daughters of Troy" puts the following lines in the mouth of Andromache:

> Mother, O mother, a fairer, truer word
> Hear / that I may with solace touch thine heart:
> To have been unborn I count as one with death
> But better death than life in bitterness

The death wish is given ample expression in the Old Testament. It comes from some of God's greatest servants. There is Elijah, who, after his dramatic victory over the prophets of Baal on Mount Carmel flees to Mount Sinai to escape the wrath of Jezebel. Sitting under a broom tree, without food or water, he says:

> It is enough; now, O LORD, take away my life,
> for I am no better than my ancestors.
> (1 Kgs 19:4)

Earlier it was King David, weeping in solitude after hearing the news that Absalom has been killed, crying out:

> O my son Absalom, my son, my son Absalom!
> Would I had died instead of you. O Absalom,
> my son, my son!"
> (2 Sam 18:33)

Then there was Jeremiah and Job, who cursed the day they were born, and the self-centered Jonah who wanted to die after preaching successfully in Nineveh, but unhappy because God would not destroy the city after it repented.

The wish to die or never to have lived is not restricted to people of antiquity. In the 1920s, when life for many in America was traveled in the "fast lane," others were hurt and broken. The chorus of a popular song on Broadway giving vent to the hurt of a wounded lover went:

"It Is Finished!"

> I wish I had never seen sunshine
> I wish I had never seen rain
> I wish that your soul had not been my goal
> A prize that I sought all in vain
> I only wish someone had told me
> The love that you gave was untrue
> And I wish I had died in my cradle
> Before I grew up to love you.[2]

I have also heard more than a few melancholy Swedes sigh that deep sigh in their last years—whether it be a longing for heaven, a release from earth, or maybe some of both—and with that sigh say the words, "Would that I could go." I have stood by the bedside of people, or sat across the room from them, and heard these words. In some cases the longing to die is deep and sustained; in others it is a passing phenomenon, somewhat like the despair of Jonah forgotten once the plant grew up to give him shade.

I think, however, that there had to be conviction in Jesus' words. He spoke with a voice of confidence, assured of the fact that he had endured the struggle and made it through to the end. These were words of victory! They were strong words of a runner who had run the race and won. We are looking at a man whose cup was full, not empty, affirming his life in the fullest sense. I think we find an echo in Paul, who nearing the end of life, says to Timothy:

> As for me, I am already being poured out as a libation, and the time of my departure has come. I have fought the good fight, I have finished the race, I have kept the faith.
> (2 Tim 4:6–7)

Jesus had fought the good fight; he had kept the faith. It was finished! AMEN

---

2. (New York: Shapiro, Bernstein, 1926).

20

"Father, Into Your Hands I Commend My Spirit"[1]

Text: Luke 23:46

Then Jesus, crying with a loud voice, said, "Father, into your hands I commend my spirit." Having said this, he breathed his last

ACCORDING TO LUKE'S GOSPEL, these were Jesus' last words before he died. Luke says he cried "with a loud voice." Upon hearing the words, a Roman centurion standing by said, "Certainly this man was innocent." Jesus had already expressed intense loneliness and alienation from God. Now comes trust and submission—submission even to death. Jesus puts himself completely in the hands of God. His words once again are from the Psalms, this time Psa 31:5.

A famous study has been done by Elisabeth Kübler-Ross on the stages through which a dying person passes. The study shows that quite typically people begin, after first learning that they are going to die, by expressing anger. At the end, however, they come to acceptance. Giving in to death is a struggle. At first one does not want to admit it, then when reality sets in, one becomes angry.

1. Lenten Meditation at the Covenant Church of Menominee, MI, on April 8, 1993.

"Father, Into Your Hands I Commend My Spirit"

Only after the anger has been let out can one come to the place where they can accept death, which leads finally to peace.

One may see in these words of Jesus a final acceptance of death. But there is more. Jesus is not just submitting to the inevitable, nor is he only coming to peace. Both are occurring. But he is committing himself into the hands of God, his Heavenly Father. These words from the cross are traditionally taken to be Jesus' "reunion" with God. It is fitting that he should come to this place, for he has talked all along about going to the Father, about preparing a place for us in the Heavenly Kingdom, about then coming back to receive us unto himself. These words are very reassuring to hear, for they leave *us* at peace, knowing that before Jesus breathed his last he gave himself completely over to God in trust and submission, letting the Giver of life also be Taker of the same.

This should be an inspiration to us all, for if we know that Jesus was able to die trusting God, we can do the same. Paul captured the spirit in these words to the church at Rome:

> For I am convinced that neither death, nor life,
> nor angels, nor rulers, nor things present, nor
> things to come, nor powers, nor height, nor
> depth, nor anything else in all creation, will
> be able to separate us from the love of God in
> Christ Jesus our Lord.
> (Rom 8:38–39) AMEN

Easter

21

"If Christ Be Not Risen..."[1]

Text: 1 Corinthians 15:14, 17-18

And if Christ be not risen, then is our preaching in vain, and your faith is also vain. . . . and if Christ be not raised, your faith is vain; ye are yet in your sins. Then they also which are fallen asleep in Christ are perished

I HAVE ON MY shelf three King James Versions of the Bible. Two were presented by the North Park Covenant Church in Chicago. The first was given to me at Christmas by my Grandma and Grandpa Ohlson. I was 8 years old, and remember the occasion. I was excited because it had all of Jesus' words in red; but, as I hastened to point out to my mother when I showed it to her, my name was in gold on the front. The Bible had pictures, so I could see how people and places mentioned in the Old and New Testament looked. I don't remember exactly when I was given my second KJV Bible, but the date in the front indicates that I was 8, going on 9. This Bible was presented by Mr. P. Raymond Nelson, Superintendent of the North Park Covenant Sunday School. It also contained pictures, but Jesus' words were not in red.

---

1. Preached in the Covenant Church of Menominee, MI, on April 11, 1993.

You Are the Light of the World

My third KJV Bible is perhaps the most precious. It was given to me by the church after one year of Confirmation. It is very thin, printed on high quality paper. My pastor, the Rev. A. Eldon Palmquist, chose for me the scripture verse in II Timothy 2:15: "Study to shew thyself approved unto God, a workman that needeth not to be ashamed, rightly dividing the word of truth." Just last evening I took this Bible off the shelf to see how it translated the verses I would use this morning as my text. It used the old English subjunctive, "If Christ *be* not risen," a tense expressing something contrary to fact, now lost in modern English. I am thus using the KJV translation this morning since I think it is better.

When opening this Bible I discovered another reason why it has become special. Inside the back cover I taped a drawing given me many years ago by a 90-year old woman named Mrs. Behrens, a regular attender at church on Sunday morning. Few people knew anything about her; she had no family or close friends in the church; she just appeared one Sunday and had kept coming. But everyone knew she was there, because for some reason she always claimed a seat behind the post where her vision was impaired. We called her "the lady who sat behind the post." No one asked her why she wanted to sit there. All we knew was that she always did.

I got to know Mrs. Behrens because our pastor learned that she lived simply in an apartment down on Belmont Avenue, and had very little. He suggested that our Hi League visit her and bring her a box of food. Well, we did, and she became for me a good friend. She gave me a drawing on Easter, 1958, which said in Swedish: "En välsignad Påsk" (A blessed Easter), below which she had penciled a cross and written Joh. 19, 30 ("It is finished"). Two angels flanked the cross, and at the bottom was a blessing for me and my sister, reminding us that "Jesus lever" (Jesus lives). I remember being very moved when she gave me the drawing, enough so that I taped it in the back of my Bible. I can still hear the spoken blessing, in her frail, broken, Swedish voice.

It is Easter again, and the message we proclaim is the same as that proclaimed by the angel at the tomb, later by the women and the disciples who went to the tomb, by others who did not see the tomb empty—including Paul, and by those who had personal visitations from the resurrected Lord. To these we can add the countless numbers, which, up until this day, have preached the "good news" of Easter morning: "He is risen! The Lord Jesus is risen from the dead."

The story as told in the Bible is an incredible one: Pilate ordering that the tomb be guarded so the disciples would not steal Jesus' body and tell people he had risen from the dead (Matt 27:64–66). Then the rolling away of the large stone, perhaps by an earthquake. But even more incredible is the empty tomb for which no explanation is offered, except the one at the heart of our proclamation: He is risen! The women and the disciple disbelieved at first, afraid to receive the news and tell others, although later they did. Then the appearances of Jesus, surrounded by mystery and surprise for all who experienced them. The proclamation of the resurrection comes forth in all clarity in the Scripture, yet no attempt is made to cover over the doubt and early disbelief.

We may therefore ask, "Is it all true?" Did this miracle, this victory over hostile forces both Jew and Roman, this resurrection from the dead really happen? Perhaps we have been deluded, as on other occasions when earnest claims have been put before us.

Shocking as such thoughts might be, the Apostle Paul has us think them. In his letter to the church at Corinth he says, not once but twice, "If Christ be not risen . . ." The statement almost translates into a question, "If Christ be not risen, what then?" The words are blunt, particularly to a congregation, which, in all likelihood, had gathered to hear his letter in worship. There are four consequences that follow, and I want you to consider them with me this morning as we rethink the Easter message.

If Christ be not risen, then is our preaching in vain. This strikes at the heart of what I am doing today and any other Sunday morning that I preach. It strikes at the heart of what other preachers are doing today and on other days. It deals each of you a blow as well, for when you hear preaching, sometimes you are moved, sometimes deeply moved, and sometimes you act on what you have heard preached, and your life, not to mention the lives of others, is changed. But if Christ has not been raised, then all this preaching has been in vain. It is nothing, and you can forget about it. Changed lives are nothing. Any good coming from this talk is an accident, or a delusion. And for me, I have given my entire life to what does not exist—sacrifices made, tears shed, prayers uttered, songs played and sung over and over again; it all adds up to nothing, and my life and the life of other preachers will in the end be an enormous waste. If Christ be not risen then is our preaching in vain.

And if Christ be not raised, your faith is vain. All the trust you have put in God over the years—one gigantic mistake; all the uplifting words spoken to you in moments of struggle, all the kind deeds, the meals brought to your home, the help from neighbors on short notice, help with your children, rescues along the road when you were helpless and vunerable—by Christians or those not Christian—these, and other experiences that have rekindled your faith, simply chance happenings or events on which you have placed too much importance—none faith producing.

And those things earlier in the life of Jesus that brought people to faith, what about them? Was their faith also in vain. Was the faith of people healed by Jesus' miracles, the hearers of his Sermon on the Mount and his great parables, all in vain?

During the Middle Ages it is said that King Clovis, a barbarian and not a Christian, was listening to the story of Jesus' suffering and death and when it progressed to the point where his death was recounted, Clovis suddenly reached for his sword, drew it, and said, "Oh, if only I had been there with my Franks! We'd have charged up the slopes of Calvary and smashed those Romans and saved him."

God, however, was there. But if he had done nothing and let Jesus remain in the grave, what then? Would we have faith in a God doing less than a barbarian king? If Christ had not been raised our faith would be in vain. How long do you think you could live without faith? It would take but a few experiences of your faith being shattered to convince you that you could not live for long, for if you were not shaking you would be fearful and scared of what might happen next.

But if Christ is risen from the dead, your faith in God is crowned, and even in the blackest of days you know your life is safe in him. One of Luther's enemies is reported to have sneered at him, "Tell me, when the whole world turns against you—Church, State, princes, people—where will you be then?" "Where shall I be then?" cried the mighty warrior, "why then as now, in the hands of Almighty God!"

And if Christ be not raised . . . ye are yet in your sins. All our talk about being forgiven is nothing; all our talk about God drowning our sins in the depth of the sea and making us white like snow is nothing. Christ is neither savior of the world nor our savior. Do we worry about forgiveness? You bet we do. We worry to death about it, sometimes crying bitterly if just one wretched soul will not forgive us. We cannot live without forgiveness, for if that goes, peace goes, freedom goes, happiness goes, heaven goes, and in a moment we are at the door of despair.

Thomas Carlyle, the British writer, has a passage about a man who tries to run away from his shadow. He turns around again and again, and still it is there. Finally he says, "God, God, I can't get away from it! I can't!" That is sin without forgiveness, a dark shadow always with us that we cannot escape. In no time it will make us paranoid.

King Herod slew John the Baptist, and some months later when he heard about Jesus he said it must be John the Baptist *redivivus*, the man I killed come back from the dead (Matt 14:1–2; Mark 6:16). He could not get away from his evil deed because there was no forgiveness. Now, at the sight of anyone who reminded him of what he had done, he was afraid.

We become troubled about people who do not forgive, and it is true, such people give us pain. But let us not forget the many who have forgiven us and let our past misdeeds lie. The church, despite its imperfections, is a company of people who do more forgiving than any other community on earth. But if Christ has not been raised, we live still in our sins.

If Christ has not been raised . . . then also those who have died in Christ have perished. Think of this, those who have departed from us, precious souls of exemplary faith who have entered what we call the Church Triumphant, all these blown out as a candle. Macbeth would then be right when he says:

> Tomorrow, and tomorrow, and tomorrow
> Creeps in this petty pace from day to day
> To the last syllable of recorded time
> And all our yesterdays have lighted fools
> The way to dusty death
> Out, out, brief candle!

And what about those testimonies to faith we have heard from people about to die, people who have caught just a glimpse of the heavenly glory, of Jesus, or the New Jerusalem as John did? Are these also delusions? If Christ has not been raised . . . then those also who have died in Christ have perished. But Paul ends with a trumpet call that is one of triumph. He says: "But in fact Christ has been raised from the dead, the first fruits of those who have died" (1 Cor 15:20). HALLELUJAH! CHRIST IS RISEN! AMEN.

22

"Work Out Your Own Faith with Fear and Trembling"[1]

Text: Philippians 2:12-13

Therefore, my beloved, just as you have always obeyed me, not only in my presence, but much more now in my absence, work out your own salvation with fear and trembling; for it is God who is at work in you, enabling you both to will and to work for his good pleasure

PAUL'S LETTER TO THE Philippian Church is distinguished by its tone of joy and gratitude. His special affection for this church stems from the fact that he established it on his second missionary journey (ca. A.D. 50), at which time he was jailed with Silas, but after an earthquake rather than flee he stayed to convert the jailer and baptize his family. This church also sent Paul money on two occasions for his needs (Phil 4:16), and he appreciated that.

Paul is now again in prison, perhaps in Rome, but maybe closer in Ephesus, and he writes as if soon he will die. Early in the letter he makes that great remark showing the depth of his faith, "For to me to live is Christ, and to die is gain" (Phil 1:21). This

---

1. Preached in the Covenant Church of Thomaston, CT, on May 24, 1987.

letter to a large extent is a parting word to a church he has "fathered," giving some final and distilled advice to his child.

Parting words can range anywhere from flip remarks to serious talks; they can plea for one to make a change in his or her life; they can be confident assurances. Nervous mothers may say, "Well, you can't go on this way forever." Unsentimental fathers may say, "Hang in there, kid."

I remember when my father left home on the way to the hospital. I did not know it would be his last walk out to the car, but I was concerned about the sudden onset of what appeared to be a serious health problem. He was perhaps too shy to say anything as he walked down the front stairs, although he did smile and say good-bye. Choked with emotion, I could only say, "We're going to miss you around here." Twice I saw him briefly in the hospital, but that remark on his leaving home was the closest I came to speaking any parting words to my father. We were on good terms, so I never wished to have said anything more. More recently I was reading a family letter sent to my grandpa's brother in Colorado Springs back in the 1920s. Uncle Winfred, who was suffering from tuberculosis had not much longer to live, and in this letter he was pleading with his sister to get her life right with the Lord while there was still time.

In antiquity people were often more formal in their parting remarks. Fathers would call children in for a blessing: Jacob and Esau were given blessings by Isaac before he died; Ephraim and Manasseh were given blessings by Jacob before he died, although in Genesis 49 Jacob blesses all his children; and Moses blesses the twelve tribes of Israel just before he dies (Deuteronomy 33). Joshua, before he dies, holds a ceremony of covenant renewal with the twelve tribes at Shechem (Joshua 24); and David, on his death bed, gives the kingship over to his son Solomon.

Paul had four admonitions for the Philippian Church: 1) Be steadfast in the faith you were taught; 2) Let there be harmony and unity in the church; 3) Be humble as Christ was humble; and 4) Work out your own salvation in fear and trembling, being as obedient to God in my absence as formerly in my presence.

"Work Out Your Own Faith with Fear and Trembling"

Paul builds on a strong relationship with this church when giving his parting words. He does not have to plead with them to give over their lives to Christ; they did that a long time ago. He does not have to emphasize putting away their own futile attempts to direct their lives and give themselves over completely to God; they have already done that. Also, authority and submission—whether to God or to him as an apostle—are not at issue. Nevertheless, if Paul is to be gone, and he will be, people in this church who have looked to him for leadership and guidance will have to look elsewhere, and that elsewhere is within themselves. He says, "work out your own salvation . . ."

I would like this morning for us to mirror ourselves in the Apostle and think about what these words might mean for us as we arrive at junctures where we must give parting words to anyone who has been under our care. We need not be at death's door, but may be in robust health with more years to live. I'm thinking about when our children go off to college; when they get married; when they are alone caring for a new baby; when they move to another part of the country; after they have been under our care while sick and are now ready to go home. Pastors have a special relationship with confirmands and other young people in the church that ends when they grow up and leave for somewhere else.

Working out your own salvation is not only attending to a basic relationship with God and Jesus Christ. It is that, but it is more, much more. It is the working out a myriad of things having to do with living life to its fullest. And I cannot think of a better parting word than this when the time comes for children and others who have depended on us to leave our charge. They need to work things out with fear and trembling, knowing that God is at work in their lives for his good pleasure.

My wife Linda and I faced this not long ago when our son David left home for the first time to spend a year with friends in Norway, then going to college the next year in California. There were a host of things he must now work out on his own. We had not ceased giving him advice; we had not ceased giving him needed financial support; we had not ceased helping him in any other way we could, but we would no longer be present, and he must now work out things largely on his own.

On a more sober note, a time will come when the end of life is in sight, and we need to give another who has depended on us a confident word about working things out on their own. If you are a grandparent, you have grandchildren who will not want you to leave them. You will be expressing trust if you tell them to work out things on their own, perhaps their all-important salvation. You may have a son or daughter needing such a word. You may have a neighbor, a friend, someone in the church who needs from now on to work out things on their own.

Of course, we should not leave off the words "in fear and trembling." This does not mean debilitating fear throwing one into panic. The words express one's humble station before God. Fear in the Bible also means "reverence," and here we are talking about reverence toward God. Paul adds, not as an afterthought, but as a confident follow-through to his advice, "for God is at work in you, both to will and to work for his good pleasure." It bears repeating that Paul is saying these words not to people new in the faith. They are established in the faith and must become mature in Christ, striking out on their own to please God with their lives.

Finally, let us think of this text as if we are the ones hearing these words from another, whether a parent, a teacher, a friend, or some other person on which we have relied. Here we may have been influenced by a theology too heavy on grace and too light on works, relying only on what God does and not on what we must do ourselves, and that can be a problem. Paul taught us much about grace and faith, but here he has a positive word about works. Jesus the same in his Sermon on the Mount (Matt 5:16).

I mentoned earlier the closing of one age with Joshua at the Shechem covenant renewal ceremony. If you read on into the Book of Judges you discover that there was a serious vacuum after Joshua's death. This dark perod is summed up in Judg 21:25, where it says, "all the people did what was right in their own eyes." Yes, there were some good judges like Gideon, who stepped forward in faith and brought deliverance to Israel, and also a few others, but

"Work Out Your Own Faith with Fear and Trembling"

it was otherwise not a happy period in Israel's history. Gideon has always been a favorite for Sunday School lessons. He was uncertain about moving ahead; one sign was not enough, he needed another. Finally God assurred him he could win the battle. And he did.

One of the reasons for the surge of dogmatic and authoritarian movements in our own day—whether they be Christian or of another sort—has to do with the timidity and immaturity of people who are unable to work out their own salvation in the way Paul envisioned. We cannot remain as children, waiting always to be told to do this or do that. Yes, the NT teaches us to become as children, but that has to do largely with the faith children typically possess. We must become mature Christians, and we do this by working out our own salvation with fear and trembling, for God is at work in us, enabling us to will and work for his good pleasure. AMEN

Pentecost

23

"When I Was a Child"[1]

Text: 1 Corinthians 13:11

When I was a child, I spoke like a child, I thought like a child, I reasoned like a child; when I became a man, I gave up childish ways

PAUL WAS ONCE A child, and his recollection of childhood is prompted by what he said two verses preceding about knowledge and prophecy being imperfect. His words:

> For our knowledge is imperfect and our prophecy is imperfect; but when the perfect comes, the imperfect will pass away (1 Cor 13:9–10 RSV)

The key words are "perfect" (τέλειον) and "imperfect" (μέρους). The Greek, however, does not denote in "perfect" the sense of flawless, or "imperfect" as having a blemish. The basic ideas are completeness or incompleteness, fragmented or being whole. The NRSV here is better. Paul is saying that our knowledge and prophecy are not complete; they remain fragmented until what completes it comes along. So when Paul talks of speaking, thinking,

---

[1]. Preached in the Covenant Congregational Church of Boston, on June 15, 1975.

and reasoning like a child, he is recalling the fragmentation characterizing childhood.

A child's speech is characterized by fragmentation. It happens in any language, but perhaps more so in English because the language is so irregular. My four-year old girl says: "Mommy readed the book to me." You can all remember things your children or grandchildren said that were incorrect. One might say they were just wrong, but they were also the result of a fragmented knowledge of the language.

A child's thinking and reasoning are fragmented. We are often mistaken in saying that a child cannot think or reason. Children can think and reason very well, but are limited in both because they either do not have all the pieces or have not put all the pieces together. The dean at my seminary tells of what happened to his young daughter when she together with her mother and two older sisters were forced to evacuate India. Young Jennie was very close to her father, more than the others, and after they left dad behind Jenny talked a good bit about him. She missed him.

The family returned to Australia, and six months later dad rejoined them. Everyone was happy to see him, except Jennie. She wouldn't even look at him, and for weeks quietly kept her distance. Finally, one evening she came and sat on his lap, and gradually the two came close. What apparently happened was that for Jennie the dear father left behind never came back, and in his place came another man. Everyone was glad to see dad again except Jennie. Her young mind had been unable to put things together.

I heard another story last weekend on the lighter side about little Ben Rooker. Mother Irene had gone to New York and my wife said to Ben on Sunday, "I hear your mother is in New York." Ben shook his head "No." Linda said, "Yes, she went to New York for the weekend." Ben still said "No." "Well, then, where is she?" Ben said, "She's down at the bus station." No problem with logic, just a fragmented picture of what had happened. He was reasoning like a child.

My nine-year old son learned for the first time last weekend when we went to the top of the Prudential Building and saw the

"When I Was a Child"

broadcasting studio of an FM radio station that music on the radio came off of records. "When I was a child, I spoke like a child, I thought like a child, I reasoned like a child, but when I became a man..."

But Paul became a man. And when this happened he says he gave up childish ways. I suppose we could imagine that Paul gave up a multitude of things, but in this context it is clear that what Paul gave up was the fragmented views of childhood. Becoming a man meant getting it all together. Paul was able to unite churches split between Jews and Greeks; he was able to integrate his Jewish understanding of the law with Jesus' teachings of grace and forgiveness. The early Church was not a homogeneous group, and had not Paul been someone who was himself put together he could never have succeeded in pulling the Church together.

One can scarcely think of what might have happened had there not been a Paul to lead the early Church. Hear what Paul says in the chapter just prior to the present one, where he first talked about a variety of gifts but just one Spirit (1 Cor 12:4–11), and then went on to say:

> For just as the body is one and has many members, and
> all the members of the body, though many, are one body,
> so it is with Christ. For in the one Spirit we were all
> baptized into one body—Jews or Greeks, slaves or free—
> and we were all made to drink of one Spirit
> (1 Cor 12:12–13)

Paul goes on to show that parts of the body cannot function independently, but must work together. So it is with the church: its members have their various gifts, but they must work together (vv 14–31). This understanding came when Paul became a man!

Paul was not a father, although he was like a father to the churches he established. Thus everything we have said about him becoming a man could equally apply to becoming a good father. Being a good father means giving up fragmented views of childhood and getting things together. Running debates between father and child are often caused because both hold fragmented views. The father wants the child to do something the way he did it when he was a child, and the child has a different idea. It thus becomes a debate between two individuals both of whom are still children in their thinking. The father must become a man; not remain as a child. If he does not, the child will have to seek out an uncle, a grandfather, or some other adult to defragmentize his or her world.

Having more than one child helps broaden our understanding. We find that what worked well with one child does not work well with the other. Finally, we come to realize that children are different. And so they are. But we should ponder the fact that because they are different we need to break out of our own stereotypes inherited from childhood. As men we should talk to other men about being a father. The same goes for women; they need to talk to other mothers, and usually they do. In fact, I think they do a better job of this than men, who rarely talk to other men about their children. They talk about work, golf, baseball, cars, and maybe politics, but rarely about children. This may explain why some have fragmented ideas about fathering.

The Church, I believe, gives us a good context in which to become defragmentized, another reason why it is so important to have men in the church. All too often they do not come. When they do come, they are more a man, not less.

Another point Paul makes in this great love chapter of 1 Corinthians 13 is undeclared. He says that our knowledge and prophecy remain imperfect; that we still see as in a mirror dimly; that we know only in part. This is another way of saying that *we yet remain as children!* Paul speaks this way to the Corinthians because his own conversion is not too far in the past, also because people in the Corinthian church are new in the faith. Hear what he says earlier in the letter:

> And so, brothers and sisters, I could not speak to you
> as spiritual people, but rather as people of the flesh,
> as infants in Christ. I fed you with milk, not solid food,
> for you were not ready for solid food. Even now you
> are still not ready (1 Cor 3:1–2)

Only later in the letter does Paul speak about maturity. And he will talk about maturity in other letters (e.g., Eph 4:13–14). Paul knows that in the Christian walk one must grow from being babes to being mature men and women. We do this by becoming defragmentized. The young must get together with the old; old women must get together with young women; young men must get to know older men. The mix will edify each and the entire church body. AMEN

24

Pilgrims Here, Settlers There[1]

Text: Luke 12:15

And he said to them, "Take care! Be on your guard against all kinds of greed; for one's life does not consist in the abundance of possessions"

ON A VISIT TO birthplaces of two of my grandparents in Sweden a few years ago, I saw their humble dwellings and reflected on why they and their families left home to come to America. Neither left because of religious persecution, and I am not even sure that my grandmother's family left Småland in the late 1880s because of the current famine in that part of Sweden. Perhaps they did; but from the stories I've heard, and from what I have read since, it is likely they wanted to come to America to acquire land and work it for themselves. They may also have had a desire for adventure as so many Swedes did in the late 19th century.

My grandmother's family, for many years, was in the employ of a wealthy family named Ribbing. My great, great grandfather was a coachman for Lady Ribbing, and my great grandfather a crofter, which is a farmer who leased a house and small parcel of land from its owner in exchange for his labor.

1. Preached in the Covenant Church of Menominee, MI, on July 4, 1993.

Pilgrims Here, Settlers There

My great, great grandfather on my grandfather's side was a poor farmer in Skåne, the southernmost province of Sweden. Among surviving family papers is a notice from the newspaper, dated January 14, 1884, just a year after the family left for America, which announced an auction after his death. The notice reads:

> By auction which will be held next Friday the 18th at 11:00 a.m., the remains of the deceased, pensioner Ola Gullberg, will be sold in Halleberga, consisting of copper, iron, and wooden items, a bed, linen and clothes, furniture, and one heifer. Legitimate buyers are granted three months to pay. Ola Nilsson

In America both families acquired land. My grandmother's family purchased a small farm near Boone, Iowa. My grandfather's family settled in Kewanee, IL, living in town and acquiring land in town.

I remember my grandfather telling me about the land he owned in Kewanee. It seems he and his father had a number of lots, some with houses on them. But a depression hit Kewanee following the development of Gary as the new steel city in the Midwest, with businesses and people moving out of Kewanee by the hundreds. As a result the land became worthless. About 1900 or so my grandpa put his paint store in a boxcar and moved with his brother, who had tuberculosis, to western Texas. He left his land behind, just as his father did a generation earlier.

When I was in graduate school at the University of California, Berkeley, a law professor once told a group of us that land was the best and most secure investment one could make, with one exception, and that was during a time of war. If you had to move you couldn't take it with you.

Large numbers of people—indeed whole nations—know this. In the former Yugoslavia people will tell you they had to leave most of what they had—including land—behind. And at the root of the Arab-Israeli conflict is a claim to the land—land formerly called Palestine but now called Israel, its ancient name. Arabs will say they are not hostile to Jews, but to Zionism, the movement begun early in the century whose purpose it was to secure a homeland for Jewish people. In 1948 that movement led to the expulsion of the British, a brief war with the Arabs who had occupied the land for over 1000 years, then a Jewish possession of the land. This was the first time Jews possessed a homeland since A.D. 70, when the Romans destroyed Jerusalem and sent them—along with many Christians—into all parts of the world.

Arabs have been unwilling to accept the fact that Jewish people are now in possession of the land. As a result, Arabs (or Palestinians) who fled their homes in 1948 were not allowed to assimilate into other Arab countries where they became refugees. They were kept in camps, and were it not for the United Nations they would not have had food to eat. In Lebanon these people became virtual prisoners in camps near the airport and elsewhere for almost 30 years! They could not get Lebanese citizenship; they could not get jobs; their children could not go to school, and they had no hope of living a normal life like other citizens of Lebanon. To let them assimilate would be to admit that Israel had taken their land, and the Arabs would not do this. These people had fled and could not take the land with them. Their plight was then exactly opposite of those who left Sweden and other countries of Europe and found land awaiting them in America.

Those coming first to America called themselves Pilgrims, but today we celebrate the day they appropriated land for themselves. On the one hand they had to declare independence from Great Britain, and on the other they had to wrest land from the Indians, which took another 100 years.

Linda and I visited Fort Buford on the Upper Missouri where it meets the Yellowstone—near the North Dakota-Montana border. Here Sioux Chief Sitting Bull surrendered to the Union forces a little over 100 years ago. Fifty years earlier, on July 4, 1838, Chief Blackhawk made his last speech at Fort Madison, IL to those who had taken his land. In it he said:

> A few summers ago I was fighting against you.
> I did wrong perhaps, but that is past. It is buried.
> Let it be forgotten. Rock River was a beautiful
> country. I loved my towns, my cornfields, and

the home of my people. I fought for it. It is now
yours. Keep it as we did

And so the land has become ours, and we sing:

> This land is your land
> This land is my land
> From California to the New York Islands
> From the redwood forests to the Gulf Stream waters
> This land was made for you and me

Was this land made for you and me? We like to think it was.

Ideas about the land we possess have roots in the Old Testament as early American documents show. For generations of immigrants America was a new Promised Land. The Indians were the Canaanites whom the Lord pushed out in order to give us this land.

In the Bible it was to Abraham that God promised land. Abraham, however, was only a pilgrim when he first visited this land. His descendants would receive it as an inheritance. And the day came when Joshua and his army crossed the Jordan to take possession of this land. The book of Deuteronomy gave Israel a perspective on the land. It reminded people that the land was a gift, and Israel could keep it only so long as it obeyed God's commands. If it ceased to obey, thinking it could have the land anyway, it would learn to its sorrow that God would expel it from the land just as he expelled the Canaanites earlier. That day came in 586 B.C., and it was a bitter one. Jewish people went into exile in faraway Babylon. They couldn't take the land with them.

We learn from Jesus that, like Abraham, we are but pilgrims in the land. We are given no security about land, nor indeed about any other of our possessions. To the man in our text eager to get his inheritance, Jesus responds with a chilling story about one who gets land and money, and then, as he is about to expand his holdings, finds out that his life is to be rolled up as a scroll that very night.

We had a neighbor at our summer cottage in Spread Eagle, WI to whom much the same happened. He was a top executive in a large Chicago plumbing company, and together with his wife had just spent a lot of money making their cottage into an elegant year-around home, landscaping the grounds, planting grass, which was unheard of those days among those who had summer cottages, and filling the beach with sand. The work was almost done, but not quite. Then the news came that our friend and three other company executives were killed in a plane crash in Wisconsin. We commented on what a tragedy it was, particularly in light of all the work spent getting their place redone. He could not enjoy it. Nor could he take his beautiful estate with him. You know people, too, who have invested heavily in things of this earth, and suddenly they are gone, others being left with what they accumulated. Or there are those who live on who find it impossible to give up land or home even when they are no longer able to care for either.

There are times I wish I had just a small piece of land with a cottage. I don't know if it will ever happen. But I have, in any case, become reconciled to the fact that we are pilgrims here and settlers there—"there" being that land of promise awaiting Christians after the sojourn in this land is complete. The Letter to the Hebrews says, "For here we have no lasting city, but we are looking for the city that is to come" (Heb 13:14).

There can be a kind of madness about land, possession, and other riches. We see it in individuals as well as in nations, that insatiable appetite for more and more, and a mistaken idea that we can never lose what we have. Do we not know that we can't take it with us? It is time to return to the biblical notion that all of what we have is a gift—our land in America, our freedoms, our prosperity from hard work, which is also a gift from God.

On this 4th of July let us be both thankful and humble. What we have is a gift that can be taken from us. Better that we give some of what we have away, which is what Jesus tells us a few verses later:

> Do not be afraid, little flock, for it is your Father's good pleasure to give you the kingdom. Sell your possessions, and give alms. Make purses for yourselves that do not wear out, an unfailing treasure in heaven, where no thief comes near and

no moth destroys. For where your treasure is, there your heart will be also (Luke 12:32–34).
AMEN

25

"You Are the Salt of the Earth"[1]

Text: Matthew 5:13

You are the salt of the earth; but if salt has lost its taste, how can its saltiness be restored? It is no longer good for anything, but is thrown out and trampled under foot

THIS MORNING I WANT to speak about the first of two metaphors Jesus uses after completing his "beatitudes"—a metaphor, which, like the one following, is directed to his disciples to show what discipleship ought to be like: "You are the salt of the earth."

What is meant by this teaching? We can begin by pointing out that "earth" means the same as "world" in the next teaching: "You are the light of the world." It does not mean earth in the sense of "ground," for salt has no value to the ground; in fact, it destroys the ground, as the Bible points out elsewhere (Deut 29:23; Psa 107:34). In antiquity it was common to punish a defeated enemy by sowing salt in its land. The poetic nature of Jesus' Sermon requires parallel words, which is why "earth" is used here. The meaning is "You are the salt in the world." Augustine translated: "You are the salt among the people of earth."

---

1. Preached in the Covenant Church of Thomaston, CT, on July 19, 1987.

"You Are the Salt of the Earth"

Jesus' disciples are to be salt of the earth. We first need to ask ourselves what it means to be "salt," or what are the qualities of salt and how is salt used? Salt for us is a staple, as it was also for people in antiquity. The Talmud says, "The world cannot exist without salt."

Salt has two important functions. One is the more obvious: it is a seasoning for food. Ancient people liked salt for seasoning just as we do. Cereal offerings were seasoned with salt, for the added reason that the covenant with God contained salt (Exod 30:35; Lev 2:13; Num 18:19). Job says, "Can that which is tasteless be eaten without salt?" (Job 6:6). People today on salt-free diets can tell us what it is like not to have salt on food.

The other function of salt is as a preservative. Before the days of refrigerators and freezers salt is what kept meat and other foods from spoiling. It may also have been a purifier as when Elisha made bad water good with salt (2 Kgs 2:19–22). We learn, too, from Ezekiel about the custom of rubbing newborns with salt (Ezek 16:4). This was probably for cleansing, although it could have been for some other medical purpose.

It is probably because of salt's preservative nature that the Old Testament speaks of a "covenant of salt" (Num 18:19; 2 Chr 13:5), meaning a covenant that is permanent. The Arabs have an expression, "There is salt and bread between us," which is similar. This signifies a relationship that is intimate and intended to last.

As one might expect, metaphorical meanings for salt focus on seasoning and preserving. Jesus' statement could then mean that without his disciples the world would be both insipid and corrupt. We recall that ten righteous persons could have saved Sodom (Gen 18:32). Like salt, Christians are essential for the world's well-being. Along these same lines, salt is taken as being "distinctive," which is to say that Christians must somehow be different from others in the world. Even Pliny, the pagan Roman naturalist, said, "for the whole body nothing is more beneficial than salt and sun" (*Nat. Hist.* 31:45). He then went on to discuss various uses of salt to preserve the body from corruption, and also its use as a medicine.

Is it true that Christians are a seasoned people in a world of insipid individuals? If Jesus had seasoning in mind, then this might be intended. But is it true? I would say, "Yes and no." I have been with Christians who are dull, lacking in imagination, immune to adventure, given to language lacking vigor and uninteresting. They compare poorly with more worldly types who are quite the opposite and fun to be with.

On the other hand, I would also say that the most seasoned people I have known are Christians, people who must be salty because they possess all the traits dull individuals lack. Even compared with the interesting people of the world, they are superior. Why? Largely because their joy is deeper. Even when they grieve we see joy and sorrow mingling, as Johan Brun's 18th c. Swedish hymn says:[2]

> In heaven all is gladness—Here troubles press, and fears
> Here often bowed and sighing, I eat "the bread of tears"
> Here joy and sorrow mingle, For Christ's beloved bride
> But 'tis not so up yonder, For there doth joy abide

Such people possess an inner quality corresponding to what shows on the outside. And their saltiness lasts; it is not just a passing mood disappearing as quickly as it came. Everything about salty Christians comes across as being more real.

Compare the best church gathering you can think of with the best cocktail party or social affair you attended with friends from school or work. I have been at both, and for me there is no comparison. Recall the best evening you had with Christian friends with the best evening you had with people who were not Christians, and again, how do they compare? Recall the best church wedding, Christian funeral or memorial service you have attended, and tell me how these compare with other such gatherings. I have found again and again that Christians offer something others do not have, which is, perhaps, their salt.

---

2. "In Heaven All Is Gladness," *The Hymnal of the Evangelical Covenant Church of America* (Chicago: Covenant Press, 1950), #510.

"You Are the Salt of the Earth"

I have mentioned qualities in people that may be more like fizz in soda or energy in a chocolate bar. Luther focused on "straight talk" felt necessary to denounce wrongdoing and godlessness. He talked about the "bite" a preacher must have in order to preach Christ and the Word, which is a wake-up call for all of us who preach. Luther said if the Christian preacher was not prophetic, that is, not denouncing scandals and speaking against present godlessness in the world, also in the church, and instead telling people they were doing just fine, that preacher would be like salt that had lost its taste and was therefore worthless.

I have heard such preaching, and so have you. Yet people love preachers never lacking in a positive message: "I'm OK, you're OK; God loves you, and so do I; God is going to do something real good for you today." Such preachers have huge followings, bring in huge offerings, and are very popular. It has always been so. But the prophets of old would rise up to condemn such preaching. And Luther, were he here today to weigh in on such preaching, would thunder against it. Jesus, too, would have had a harsh word for those preaching only a "success gospel." His preaching had compassion, but it also had bite. We have been talking here about preachers, but the same applies to all Christians. Paul tells the Colossians, "Let your speech always be gracious, seasoned with salt" (Col 4:6).

It is perhaps more clear that Christians, by being salt, are to be a preservative in the world; without them the world would quickly come to destruction. This idea was developed by early Christian writers, e.g., in the second century *Epistle to Diognetus*, chapters 5–6. If we ask what makes Christians preservatives in the world, the answer should be clear: It is first and foremost righteous living. Here, too, Jesus' message is scandalized because people calling themselves Christian behave no better than others.

Christians who have been baptized to a new life in Christ Jesus, who have put on the new man or the new woman, who are part of the holy priesthood, who have died to sin, but who go on, as Paul says, living the old life, scheming as they always have, deliberately lying, cheating, and deceiving others, are not salty

You Are the Light of the World

Christians. We are not talking about Christians being perfect. Nor are we talking about Christians gaining a complete victory over the forces of darkness. Neither happens. We are talking about a view of the Christian life that has "no growing from one degree of glory to another," no conscious decision of the person to get on with righteous living, no repentance of sin, and no commitment to rise above sin.

If Chrstians are to keep the world from destruction, it will not be done—indeed it cannot be done—without them living out the mandate Jesus gave to get on with quality living, whatever that might mean. Too many Chrstians say they are doing their best and make excuses for the rest. Too many scandalize Christ because they are not as upright as other people. It is an old problem and a problem yet today.

As I said before, comparisons between some Christians and people who are not Christians make it look as if the latter are salt and Christians are the ones being kept from falling into the abyss. Still, when I think of the best people I have known, they are deeply committed to Christ and make the righteousness of the world pale by comparison. They have discovered what it means to be salt of the earth. They are the salt of the earth, keeping the world from destruction.

Jesus goes on to say that if salt has lost its taste, how shall its saltiness be restored? This point has been much discussed, since it has been recognized and can now be stated with scientific certainty that pure salt cannot lose its saltiness. Various explanations have been given. Salt deposits by the Dead Sea are said to be a less pure form of salt, i.e., they are mixed with other substances. In a heavy rain their saltiness is lost. Why? Because the salt is washed away and the impure remains have no salt.

But a better explanation is that Jesus, with full awareness, is stating something contrary to fact, knowing full well that such a thing cannot happen. The idea is an absurdity, like suggesting that water might be able to lose its wetness. The same thing happens in the next teaching about disciples being a light in the world. No one in their right mind puts a lamp under a bushel. Jesus simply wants to state what the result would be if it did happen. The point here is that if salt did lose its saltiness, it would be worthless and be thrown away. It has been known a long time that salt cannot lose its saltiness. Rabbi Joshua Honan-ya (A.D. 80–131) was asked, "When salt becomes unsavory, how does it become salted?" He answered, "With the afterbirth of a mule." Question: "And is there an afterbirth of a mule?" Answer: "Can salt become unsavory?"

What is clear is the application that Jesus makes, which is neither hypothetical nor contrary to fact: Disciples could lose their saltiness, and should that happen, they would be worthless. Jesus knows his followers could lose their distinctive character, in which case their lives would be a "throw-away." Luther was also clear on this, consigning such worthless souls to the abyss of Hell.

One final point, and it is an important one. Luther said that salty living in the Sermon on the Mount must refer to everything cited in the Beatitudes: rejoicing when one is poor in spirit, when one is persecuted for righteousness' sake; allowing oneself to mourn; being meek; seeking righteousness with persistence; showing mercy; making peace—a core list for identifying salty Christians. In Mark Jesus tells his disciples, "Have salt in yourselves, and be at peace with one another" (Mark 9:50), which echoes the seventh beatitude about being peacemakers. You are the salt of the earth. Be salt of the earth. AMEN

26

"You Are the Light of the World"[1]

> Text: Matthew 5:14–16
>
> *You are the light of the world. A city built on a hill cannot be hid. No one after lighting a lamp puts it under the bushel basket, but on the lampstand, and it gives light to all in the house. In the same way, let your light shine before others, so that they may see your good works and give glory to your Father in heaven.*

THE SECOND METAPHOR JESUS uses to describe what discipleship should be like is "light." He says to them: "You are the light of the world." If salt is essential to the world, so is light. God's first creative act was to bring light into existence (Gen 1:3), and creation could not have proceeded without it. Light is an important metaphor throughout the Bible. The Psalmist says, "The LORD is my light and my salvation" (Psa 27:1). God's word is light: "Your word is a lamp to my feet, and a light to my path" (Psa 119:105). King David was said to be the lamp of Israel (2 Sam 21:17). And John in his Gospel calls Jesus "the light of the world" (John 1:4–14; 8:12). The Rabbis named Adam "Lamp of the World."

---

1. Preached at the Covenant Church of Thomaston, CT, on July 12, 1987.

"You Are the Light of the World"

Among other things, light distinguishes one thing from another; in darkness distinctions are lost. For this reason, light—like salt—is thought to give distinction, which is to say that someone who intends to be a light in the world has to be in some way distinctive. Israel in II Isaiah was to be "a light to the nations" (Isa 42:6-7; 49:6; 60:1-3), and by this was meant that it was not to be like any other nation; it was in some way to be distinctive. And Israel at its best was distinctive: It bore witness to a covenant God made with his people; to the Law and the prophets, the terms of the covenant; and finally to the Messiah, who would come to save not just Israel, but the world.

I recall being in Jerusalem in the summer of 1965, when Linda and I were on our way home from a year of study in Beirut. We had crossed through the Mandelbaum Gate to spend a week in Israel before going home. One evening we happened in upon a meeting in the King David Hotel where leaders in the Israeli government were speaking to visiting Americans, and after the meeting I got into a conversation with one of the speakers who was kind enough to invite Linda and me to walk with him down the street after leaving the hotel. We did. It was a pleasant conversation about a variety of things—Israel, the Near East, the Arabs, Zionism, the Bible, government, politics, etc., but what stuck with me after all else was forgotten, was how passionately he hoped Israel could live out its mandate to be "a light to the nations." He quoted the phrase from II Isaiah, and I knew it.

Whether Israel today has become a light to the nations is unclear. But the hope is there, and one Israeli man held to this hope. I too hold it, and I think Americans—and also many Christians—hope Israel will be a light to the nations. It happened in the past.

Our text for the morning calls upon Jesus' disciples, i.e., those of us who are his followers, to be a light in the world. Jesus says, "You are the light of the world." The question then is, "What does it mean to be the light of the world?" A basic concept associated with light is righteousness (Prov 4:18). People seeking to be a light must be righteous and must perform acts of righteousness (v. 16: "good works"). A Jewish writing says that Israel can be a light to the Gentiles / nations only if it keeps from sin (*Testament of Levi* 14:3–4). Paul tells Christians at Philippi that they must be unblemished children of God in the midst of a wicked and perverse generation, among whom they shine as "lights of the world" (Phil 2:15). But here in the Sermon of the Mount being a light is probably just like being salt, in that Jesus refers to all modes of behavior cited in the Beatitudes. Only people who so act can lighten a dark world.

But I should like this morning to emphasize light as being called to be a new, distinctive, and different people. Christians are not to be conformed to this world, lest they cease to be a light in the world; they are like a city set on a hill, a light clearly visible; and their light must be such that others will see them as being different. You perhaps have know people who have been this sort of light. There have been outstanding examples in every age, and it is helpful, I think, to look at such people more closely so as to see precisely what makes them the light Jesus is talking about.

Dietrich Bonhoeffer was a light to the world during the dark Nazi period of the 30s and 40s, and his light still shines today when shades of that terrible era come over us. Bonhoeffer is even more a light today in communist East Germany than in West Germany. Why? Because Christians there are forced to shine more than those in the West. For Bonhoeffer being a light meant not conforming to much of what he had been taught and what came to be taught later under German Socialism. His non-conformity was rooted in what Paul talks about in Romans 12: about presenting one's whole self to God as a living sacrifice; about not being conformed to the world, the nation, but rather about being transformed; not to think more highly of oneself than one ought; about beginning to exist more fully in a concrete body of Christian believers and becoming a true member of this body.

Presenting one's whole self. Bonhoeffer was raised a nominal Lutheran who felt there was defnitely a place for Christianity in one's life. He said prayers before going to bed; the family said grace before meals; Luke 2 was read on Christmas, but the family did not enter into the life of any church congregation. In 1933, when Hitler came to power, all this changed. Bonhoeffer began to attend

"You Are the Light of the World"

church regularly; he began studying the Bible and developing a devotional life; he began making political decisions on the basis of his Christian beliefs, now becoming very dangerous in Germany. But it was his journey to become a whole person. No longer was Christianity a part of life; it had become the center, and all other things were related to his being a Christian.

If you want to be a light in the world, seek to become a "whole Christian," someone who sees a connection between what the Bible teaches and the way life ought to be lived; make a connection between politics, work, recreation, paying taxes, etc.—indeed everything you do a commitment to Jesus Christ. If you put your faith together with the rest of your life you will be doing things that will surprise you, and will surprise others, and your life will be a light shining as it did not shine before.

Not being conformed to this world. This follows closely on what has just been said. For Bonhoeffer not being conformed to this world meant breaking with Hitler and National Socialism. The vast majority of Christians supported their government; Nazi flags hung in the churches. I have in my possession a picture of Hitler entertaining some Catholic nuns to their delight.

Yet two days after Hitler seized power, Bonhoeffer gave his first (and last) radio talk. It was on his concept of what a leader ought to be. Ebehard Bethge says of the speech:

> [Bonhoeffer's] theological insight enabled him to warn his listeners that, should the leader 'allow himself to succumb to the wishes of those he leads, who will always seek to turn him into their idol, then the image of the leader will gradually become the image of the "misleader" . . . This is the leader who makes an idol of himself and his office, and who thus mocks God'[2]

Bonhoeffer thus began to counsel people—especially people in his church—not to be conformed to this world: to oppose the war of national expansion; to oppose the idea of a German super

---

2. Ebehard Bethge, *Dietrich Bonhoeffer* (New York: Harper & Row, 1970), 194.

race; to oppose the burning of the Berlin synagogue and the persecution of Jews that began in November 1938.

We sometimes hear that when Jews were being persecuted in Germany no one spoke up for them. That simply is not true. There were others besides Bonhoeffer who spoke up, and they were taken to the same prison camps as the Jews. While Bonhoeffer sought not to conform to the world, which led to many friendships being terminated, and many in government becoming hostile to him, renewal came by an inner transformation: Bible reading, a devotional life, and the singing of Paul Gerhardt hymns.

What does your life look like in comparison to others in the world? Are you conforming to what is going on around you—in church, in school, in the community? If so, you will in some cases not be a light in the world. To be a light means to rise above nominal living. And nominal living today includes accepting many of the offerings on cable TV; accepting current ideas on sex, live-ins; and a host of pleasures beckoning on every front.

Not thinking too highly of yourself. Bonhoeffer was raised in an upper class environment and had the tendency to look down on people of the lower class. He first looked down on the Jews. Later he looked down on inferior American theologians while studying at Union Seminary in New York City. He looked down on the church as a bourgeois institution. But there came a point when Bonhoeffer's life became a service to all of these and it continued in latter days as he ministered to others imprisoned with him.

The church today in America is caught up in middle and upper class values. We are being told that we can be Christian and have just as much of the world's material goods and pleasures as we want. We are too busy, many of us, to be bothered with service. It is costly in terms of time. Much of our ineffectiveness as Christians stems from the fact that we think of ourselves as too important, and with this inflated view we are not lights in the world we live in. The lights are humble souls who are not above any task, however lowly, however insignificant.

Being part of the body of Christ. If Bonhoeffer was opposed to the idea of giving religion "its place" in life, he was even more opposed to living the Christian life alone. Christianity for him was personal, but never private. He knew what Luther knew, namely, that we find Christ in the faces of other people, which means life together in the church.

Perhaps one of the best ways we can be a light in the world is in living together with other people. Families living well together are lights to other families; marriages working well are a light to other married people. The same goes within the church. The better we live and work together the more we become distinctive, the more we become lights in our world. Five hundred candles make more light than one candle!

Jesus says we should be confident enough about our light-giving qualities that we be like cities set atop a hill. Our lives need to be open to public view and public scrutiny. Actually they are, and if our lights do shine, others will give glory to God, which is the important end-result. Being a light glorifies God, who in the beginning made light, and in the end wants all people to come to the light in Christ Jesus. AMEN

27

Authority from Above or Below?[1]

Text: Matthew 21:23

When he entered the temple, the chief priests and the elders of the people came to him as he was teaching, and said, "By what authority are you doing these things, and who gave you this authority?"

SINCE THE MID-1960S, I believe, we have been very conscious in America about authority, also people claiming to possess authority. Those in positions of authority, whether parents, teachers, employers, landlords, police, or government officials, decry the fact that they are not being given the authority they possess, while those under them question their authority or reject it. I think we all assume that authority comes from above, from someone over us, and that it works from the top down. When people of authority speak we are obliged to listen, and in many cases to obey. It was so in ancient Israel, where the Hebrew verb "to hear" also meant "to obey."

But in reality authority comes from both above and below. One of my seminary teachers used to tell us that authority is always earned; it is something others give you. Position can make

1. Preached in the Covenant Church of Thomaston, CT, on January 8, 1984.

AUTHORITY FROM ABOVE OR BELOW?

little or no difference. Even if you are without a position, people may still listen to you and do what you say. And if you have a position, you are less likely to lose it if you have authority from below. It is especially so in a democracy, where support from below is what brings a person into office, and the loss of that support may result in the office being given to someone else. We saw this in the 1960s, a time of severe crisis in America. People who retained their authority had it from below as well as from above. Those not having it from below lost it.

In ancient Israel some leaders possessed authority by virtue of their position. The king earned it initially because of military success, but once the authority was his, it moved from the top down. It works this way even today in the military. Saul and David were popular kings, but Solomon inherited the kingship and with him a royal line in Judah was established. Things followed a different course in North Israel, but there too, the king once chosen claimed authority with the royal office. Priests were in a line of priests, and their authority went from the top down.

With prophets things were different. Prophets had authority from above and below. Authority above was from God who called them into service. They spoke, "Thus said the Lord." No one appointed the prophets, so far as we know, and there was no line of succession as with kings and priests. At the same time prophets—at least the true prophets—achieved great standing among the people—not all, to be sure—but a significant number, and these gave them their authority. They had authority from below. Prophets gained credibility because they could fortell the future and speak candidly about what was going on in the present—both good and bad.

With the prophet Jeremiah we see times when his authority was called into question. In 609 he gave some riveting oracles in the temple about covenant disobedience (Jer 7:1–15), which are summarized with background material in Jeremiah 26. Priests, prophets, and others did not like what he was preaching, so Jeremiah was put on trial. Calls came for his death.

What was Jeremiah's defense? He said simply that the Lord had sent him to prophesy. This was his claim for authority from above. He had been called to prophesy, and what's more, the Lord told him to say what he had just said. At the same time Jeremiah was sensitive to the authority residing in the group assembled before him. He openly acknowledged it when he said, "But as for me, here I am in your hands. Do with me as seems good and right to you" (Jer 26:14).

Support from below was forthcoming. The princes and now also the people rose to his defense, saying he did not deserve to die. Certain elders present at the trial also rose to their feet, pointing out that the prophet Micah earlier prophesied doom against Jerusalem and King Hezekiah did not put him to death. Jeremiah was thus acquitted, although he needed more support from below, getting it in the person of Ahikim son of Shaphan, who kept him from any in the crowd still angry at a decision that did not go their way (Jer 26:24). Jeremiah benefited from authority vested in the people on another occasion when he faced off with the prophet Hananiah, saying that Judah must now submit to Nebuchadnezzar of Babylon. After the confrontation he was able to walk away, which means he had sufficient authority from those who were present that day as onlookers (Jeremiah 28).

In our text for the morning, Jesus is being asked about his authority, whether he had any warrant to preach in the way he had been doing. His response was immediate. He answered with a question that would enable them to answer their own question. He brought up John the Baptist. Was his baptism from God or from the people? Was John sent by God, or was he just another human phenomenon? The question was difficult to answer. Why? Because if his opponents conceded that John's ministry was of God, why then did they not believe him? If they said John was just another self-made preacher, they would have to answer the masses who gave John credibility (Matt 21:25–26). John had authority from above as well as from below.

I came to the same conclusion about authority when I traveled to East Germany a month ago. Luther was someone who definitely felt he possessed authority from above. He had given up the authority of the Roman Church and found authority in Jesus Christ and the Scriptures. At the same time, Luther had authority from below. Frederick III, Elector of Saxony, along with the German people gave him broad support. Even after his defense before the Emperor at Worms, people rallied to his aid as they did for Jeremiah. He was hidden for an entire year in the Wartburg Castle.

This is a new day, and lest we become self-satisfied that we are Protestants and not Catholics, may we be reminded of the credibility of the Catholic Church in Poland during the recent crisis in that country. It is widely acknowledged, both inside Poland and out, in the West and in the East, among Christians and non-Christians, that the Catholic Church possesses authority to do what the state had been unable do to mediate the crisis.

Much the same could be said about the Lutheran Church in East Germany. That church is strong; it has credibility; it has authority not only from above, i.e., from Jesus Christ, but from below, i.e., among the people. I have seen it with my own eyes. In my judgment the church in these two communist countries, Poland and East Germany, has more authority than many churches in the West. And the difference is not so much in the authority they claim from above, but in the authority they possess from below. They have it while often we do not.

The church in East Germany learned from Dietrich Bonhoeffer that it must earn the right to speak; it must be given authority by the people. And it has done this by being a servant church, by standing up for what is right, by fighting for what is essential, not for things that do not matter or lie outside its province. This does not mean that it ceases to look at Jesus as Lord of the church. Not at all. It simply recognizes that Jesus comes to the church not only in a direct personal way, but indirectly through people—other people in the world. Jesus comes as risen Lord and in the lowly brothers and sisters of our world, some of whom are not Christian.

What authority does our local church have? This is a question we must ask ourselves. No doubt we can see areas where we do have authority in our community, where people do listen when we say something. But if we seem to be lacking in authority, we must look in both directions—both above and below. We serve Jesus as Lord; we proclaim his word; we submit to his power being at work in our lives, individually and as a church body. At the same time, another authority supports us from below. It is people standing behind us and our work because we have earned the right to speak, because we have credibility, because we are believable. That also goes for each of us as individuals. Our Christian life is measured not only by our claim to be saved by Jesus' blood, but by credibility we have in the eyes of others.

How do we achieve this? Briefly, I would just repeat three things I mentioned a moment ago in passing: 1) we must speak the truth; stand up for what is right; not be careless in handling the facts, nor silent in the face of wrongdoing; 2) we must be the servant once and a while, which means not always being in charge; now and then we need to give ourselves into the hands of others for their assessment; and 3) we must not try and be an authority in everything, because people who are authorities in everything often end up being authorities in nothing. We must learn to say, "I don't know"; we must let others guide us where they are the expert and we are not; we must save our valiant defenses for times when we know we are right.

Authority is kind of like your name. We claim it and use it to make things authoritative. At the same time, our name was given to us and is heard entirely in the mouths of others, where it can be honored or abused. To have a good name one must earn it, and with a good name comes authority from below. AMEN

28

Lessons from Greek Games[1]

Text: Philippians 2:14-15

Do all things without grumbling or questioning, that you may be blameless and innocent, children of God without blemish in the midst of a crooked and perverse generation, among whom you shine as lights in the world

I SUSPECT THE APOSTLE Paul would be most interested in the Olympic Games currently taking place in Los Angeles, for on more than one occasion in his letters we see that he was well aquainted with the Greek Games and very often appropriated metaphors from them to describe his view of the Christian life.

For Jewish people in the second century B.C. the Greek Games had a destructive influence in Jerusalem. Antiochus Epiphanes had a gymnasium built in the city and sponsored games in which Jewish people were encouraged to take part. The unhappy story is told in 2 Maccabees 4, where it says that priests went so far as to neglect sacrifices in the temple to take part in wrestling events and throwing the discus.

---

[1]. Preached in the Covenant Church of Thomaston, CT, on August 5, 1984.

Paul's views on the Games was more positive. Of course, he was the bearer of a new religion making inroads into the Greek world, and perhaps this turn of events and his confidence that the gospel he was proclaiming would overtake decadent Greek and Roman religion made the difference. At any rate, he drew often from the Games in his preaching, particularly when speaking to Gentiles in Greek cities.

Paul talks most often about the footrace. If in the Old Testament life is described as walking down the right path, for Paul it is a race run in the stadium. At the Greek city of Antioch of Pisidia, in one of his missionary sermons, he speaks about John the Baptist "finishing his course." He is talking about John running a race like those in the Olympics (Acts 13:25). Calling elders from Ephesus at Miletus, he says he counts his life of value "if only I may finish my course and the ministry that I received from the Lord Jesus" (Acts 20:24). In Galatians Paul says he went up to Jerusalem to consult with Chrstians in the church there "in order to make sure that I was not running, or had not run, in vain" (Gal 2:2), and again speaking directly to the Galatians: "You were running well; who prevented you from obeying the truth" (Gal 5:7). Later to Timothy he utters the familiar words, "I have fought the good fight, I have finished the race, I have kept the faith." Awaiting him therefore is a crown of righteousness, which the Lord, the righteous Judge, will award him and others on that day of Christ's appearing (2 Tim 4:7–8).

For Paul the Christian life is a race in which there are hindrances and opponents, and these can keep one from going on to victory. What is more, there are rules by which one must compete—something as much a part of the ancient Greek Games as in modern ones. Paul tells Timothy, "And in the case of an athlete, no one is crowned without competing according to the rules" (2 Tim 2:5). One cannot break rules in training or in competition. You cannot be "taking drugs;" you cannot make a false start off the blocks; two cautions are all you get in Greco-Roman wrestling; in a walking race you cannot run; in gymnastics you cannot land outside the mat in the floor exercises; and sometimes a certain level of difficulty is required to achieve a maximum score, and thus a win.

Lessons from Greek Games

I should like to pull out three lessons from the Greek Games this morning, lessons the Apostle Paul has given us and lessons we have learned from watching the Games in Los Angeles. The first is this: training is of ultimate importance. You do not get ready in hasty fashion to win the prize; you live a disciplined life over a long period to bring your performance to a level higher than that reached by others. We have seen TV film clips showing athletes in their training exercises—many hours a day, day after day, for months and even years. We now have a training center in Colorado Springs that has paid dividends for our athletes. The question frequently asked the athlete after the medal has been won, is "Was all the training worth it?" One young lady was asked how she felt about being kept from the normal life of a teenager. Victors all seemed to think it was worth it, and do not view training as a deprivation.

Paul says, "train yourself in godliness" (1 Tim 4:7), which is even more important than Olympic training, jogging, or aerobics. Do you think of the Christian life as one requiring training? Or do you think you can win by preparing with a supply of cold drinks and chips? Paul Holmer, professor at Yale, has written a book about living a Christian life that makes sense.[2] In his chapter on virtue, Holmer says that doing a virtuous thing once does not make one a virtuous person. What makes a virtuous person are habitual acts done in a virtuous way. One needs to be virtuous day after day. One needs to develop good habits, be honest when no one is looking, live well day after day, month after month, year after year. Only in this way can one win the crown.

Scores of people do outstanding things on a single occasion. But this is not the disciplined life Paul is talking about. Paul says athletes must exercise self-control in all things. One does not run aimlessly, nor box as though beating the air, but rather punishing the body (1 Cor 9:24–27). Actions must have an aim, a purpose; they must be controlled to bring about some final goal.

---

2. Paul Holmer, *Making Christian Sense* (Philadelphia: Westminster Press, 1984).

The second point is this: the olympic athlete is one who strains forward toward the goal, not looking back. This applies to the preparation; it applies to the actual race. Paul says, "This one thing I do: forgetting what lies behind and straining forward to what lies ahead, I press on toward the goal for the prize of the heavenly call of God in Christ Jesus" (Phil 3:13–14). A couple athletes saw their hopes of an olympic victory nearly evaporate with the boycott of the '80 Games. Rowdy Gaines, of Winter Haven, Florida, retired from swimming after the summer of 1980, but then came back to win the 100 meter free style in Olympic record time of 49.80 seconds. He also won gold on the men's relay race. He said his grandmother helped keep his dream alive. Here an older woman was looking ahead, not back. It was the same with Robert Shannon in boxing. After the '80 boycott he quit boxing for a year, but because he looked ahead he resumed training, fought to the top of his division, and was now going for the gold. Jeffrey Blatnick of Schenectady, New York, won the gold in Greco-Roman wrestling because he looked ahead and not back. He had a two-year bout with Hodgkin's Disease, took a lot of radiation, and said about his struggle, "The story of my life is that when there is a setback, I just bounce right back."

Can you say that about the race you are running? You have had a setback. Can you bounce back? If your sights are ahead, you can. If you keep looking back, you cannot. I hear so often of people telling me about past hurts. We all have them. But too many in the Christian race cannot get over them, and as a consequence they will not end up winners.

Finally: the olympic athlete, however much he or she be an individual performer, does not record only an individual victory. You take others with you when you win. We had friends in California cheering wildly for Rafer Johnson, gold medal winner of the decathlon in Rome in 1960, who took the torch from Gina Hemphill and climbed 99 steps to the top of the Los Angeles Coliseum where he waved the torch for 95,000 spectators to see, and then lit the cauldron atop the coliseum. Rafer grew up in the Covenant Church in Kingsburg, California under the ministry of Rudolph

Johnson, and brought with him many friends from there and elsewhere in the victory and subsequent honor he attained.

The town of West Springfield, Massachusetts went wild the morning after Tim Daggett scored a perfect 10 on the high bar, helping to bring gold to the United States in team gymnastics for the first time since 1904. His coaches in high school, the principal, and countless others shared the glory of Tim's performance. Steve Fraser, who won gold in cycling, said he kept going "for the people out there." Peter Vidmar, another member of the men's gymnastics team, said, "I hope there's a lot of kids out there that saw us do this and will run out to be gymnasts . . ." Carl Lewis, who won the 100 meters, said he was running for the love of the sport, for himself, for the people around him, for his country, and for the glory of God. Paul's concern was that the Philippians live blamelessly amidst a crooked generation so he "did not run in vain" for them (Phil 2:16).

Do you realize that your accomplishments bring glory to God and also great excitement to your brothers and sisters in the faith? You young people who are leaving this month for a year abroad, do not forget that you are living not just for yourselves, but for all of us, for others who ran before you, and above all for God. The church is a body in which the glories of its members are shared. We must never forget this. We share also in the glory of Christ, whose final victory we celebrate this morning in the service of Holy Communion. AMEN

29

Abraham Obeyed[1]

Text: Hebrews 11:8–10

By faith Abraham obeyed when he was called to set out for a place that he was to receive as an inheritance; and he set out, not knowing where he was going. By faith he stayed for a time in the land he had been promised, as in a foreign land, living in tents, as did Isaac and Jacob, who were heirs with him of the same promise. For he looked forward to the city that has foundations, whose architect and builder is God

AS ONE MIGHT EXPECT, Abraham appears in the roll call of Hebrews 11 as one of the great persons of faith. Following is mention of his wife Sarah, also singled out for her faith. Together they formed a faithful team in the story of God's redemption of the world. I am going to focus this morning on Abraham; next Sunday I will speak on Sarah, who in Genesis is said to have laughed when God's messenger told the two of them that she would bear a son (Gen 18:9–15).

Faith is shown in a variety of ways, as the writer of Hebrews makes plain: Abel showed faith by making a proper sacrifice (Gen

---

1. Preached in the Covenant Church of Hilmar, CA, on August 24, 1980.

4:4); Enoch's faith was seen in that God "took him," which is taken to mean that he did not see death (Gen 5:24); Noah heeded God's warning of impending judgment by building an ark (Gen 6:13–22); and Moses showed faith by rejecting Egyptian citizenship and identifying himself with an enslaved people (Exod 2:10–15; 12:50–51). But Abraham's faith is seen in that he obeyed: "By faith Abraham obeyed when he was called to set out for a place that he was to receive as an inheritance; and he set out, not knowing where he was going."

Looking back into Genesis we see that Abraham's greatness lay in the fact that God called him to set out to a new place, and he went (Gen 12:1–4). Abraham obeyed. The call in Genesis 12 is nicely contrasted with the Babel story in Genesis 11. In the Babel story men decide to build a great city with a temple. The word "tower" is misleading; the building is a ziggurat, a Babylonian temple. The motive is therefore religious. They want to make a name for themselves, while at the same time not wanting to be scattered abroad. So we have a complex of ambitions that would receive the blessing of many today: a drive to succeed, a desire to achieve fame; thoughts about security; and a religious motive. The city will be a place to worship Marduk, the Babylonian god.

But God looks down on this upward striving and disapproves. In fact, he destroys the enterprise entirely and scatters people to the four winds, exactly what they did not want. More than that, God now takes the initiative. He selects a man called Abram, who incidentally is from Ur in southern Babylonia, and without setting up a single condition he promises Abram a new land to be shown him. God will make of him a great nation; he will bless him; he will make his name great, and all people of the earth will be blessed in him.

A truly remarkable move on God's part—to select a man and give him this great promise without exacting a single commitment. All that would be required of Abram was that he obey. And that is what he did. He obeyed: "He went as the Lord told him." How simple when compared to the complex aspirations of the men of Babel. How simple when compared to complex demands today of keeping the religious establishment going, working for our security, and hoping that something we do in life will cause our name to be remembered after we die. All God asked of Abraham was that he obey.

This great truth was captured by Dietrich Bonhoeffer in his book, *Cost of Discipleship*. Bonhoeffer was concerned about the call to follow Jesus, and he looked into the Old Testament to where Abraham received his call to follow God. What Bonhoeffer discovered is that if one is to take discipleship seriously one must take obedience seriously.

We learn from the story of Abraham that one does not know prior to embarking on a journey what it will mean and where the journey will end up. For these reasons many cannot take the step of discipleship. They want to know everything before they set out. God's promise is not enough. Bonhoeffer says there are many who think that only after they come to a clear belief in God, only after they know correct doctrine, only after God lays out his will before them, can they obey. But he turns it around, saying, "only he who obeys can really believe." Only after you take the step of obedience, after you answer the call to discipleship, after you are already "down the road a piece," are you able to truly believe. True belief, confirmation of belief, and understanding the will of God come later, sometimes much later.

I remember when Linda and I were planning our first trip abroad. We were to be married in August, and then leave in two weeks for Beirut where I had applied to study a year at the Near East School of Theology. I was in the middle of seminary training at North Park Theological Seminary in Chicago. We were both pretty good at planning, and both liked to have as good an idea as possible of what was in store. So for six months we made every conceivable preparation for the journey. We believed God was leading us.

Before we left some things had not yet been taken care of, some very important things. They couldn't be. We did not know where we would live. We did not know if either of us could find work to support our stay. Linda had applied to teach at the

American Community School, but could not be hired stateside, so we would have to wait until arriving in Beirut to see if she had a job. We had money enough to stay a few months, but not an entire year. Perhaps we would have to return home in mid-year.

Well, we trusted God, whom we believed had called us to this undertaking, and we went. Even the trip to Beirut from Germany by car was in some doubt. We had secured all the help we could get from AAA, but how to get through Yugoslavia? What would the roads be like? And what about Turkey? Could we get passage through Syria? Greece and Turkey were in the midst of a crisis over Cyprus, and we would be driving through both countries. As it turned out, we passed military conveys in Greece heading toward the Turkish border, and when we crossed into Turkey, conveys of Turkish trucks were coming the other way! It was 3000 miles of adventure, and we could not be sure of getting there until we were there. But we arrived!

Getting a place to live was difficult, and for a time we didn't think we were going to succeed. But with help from the Rev. Romain Swedenburg, pastor at the American Community Church, we managed to get an apartment a half block from the Cornice and beautiful Mediterranean. It was across the street from the American Community School. Linda did get her teaching job, but only at a late hour when the teacher slated for the 6th grade failed to show up. Lebanese law, as it turned out, would not allow me to work.

What we learned from all of this was that belief—real belief—came not before we set out on our journey, and not completely while we were on the way, but only afterwards. It was true for us as it was for Abraham, and what Bonhoeffer taught us, namely that obedience to God's call, was the first and most important thing.

How much do you think Abraham knew about what lay ahead of him? God's promise was pretty general: the land I will show you (where is it?); I will make of you a great nation (how?); I will bless you (how?); I will make your name great (really?); you will be a blessing to all families of the earth (how can that be?).

You young people here this morning, some having just returned from a youth conference, others having returned from church camp: Has God called you to follow him? Has Jesus Christ called you to be his disciple? Have you sensed him taking the initiative in your life as he did with Abraham, promising great things with no strings attached? There may be some new turf ahead, some place where you can grow as his special child. Blessing may await you. Perhaps your name will become great, and if not great, you will at least be a somebody instead of a nobody. And if your life will be a blessing to others, what more could you want?

Most important is obeying God's call. This is what matters. Forget about problems not yet solved; forget about the will of God not being entirely clear. Get up and go! Obey God's voice; follow him! Maybe some of you are being called into Christian ministry, some to be missionaries. If so, God wants simply that you obey his voice. Let him do what you yourself cannot do. Forget about the big house you want to build, a good job, and financial security. Let God bring you the greatness he has in store. Your faith will be tested by obedience. AMEN

30

And Sarah Laughed[1]

Text: Hebrews 11:11

By faith Sarah herself received power to conceive, even when she was past the age, since she considered him faithful who had promised

IN THIS DAY OF a new consciousness about equality between men and women, husbands and wives, it struck me that the writer of Hebrews is exceedingly evenhanded in treating traditions about Abraham and Sarah, at least according to most Bible translations. In the majority of modern Versions (Tyndale; KJV; RSV; JB; NAB; NEB; REB), Sarah is given credit for her faith (v 11). The NIV and NRSV, however, follow another ancient reading that expands Abraham's faith: "By faith he received power of procreation, even though he was too old," adding parenthetically "and Sarah herself was barren."

When we look back into Genesis we find no passages speaking of Sarah's great faith. If anything, she is treated with amusement, if not in an uncomplimentary way, as for example, when divine messengers on their way to carry out the destruction of

---

1. Preached in the Covenant Church of Hilmar, CA, on August 31, 1980.

Sodom stop by the oaks of Mamre to give Abraham and her the news that she will bear a son in the spring (Gen 18:1–15).

Actually, the entire account in Genesis 18 is told in a humorous vein. Regarding Sarah, the messengers ask where she is. Abraham says she is in the tent. Do they want her to come out? Apparently not. Why then did they ask for her? The announcement about her bearing a son is given to Abraham. Do they speak loudly enough so Sarah will hear?

Well, she does hear, for we are told that she was listening behind the flaps of the tent. Those outside are also listening, for they hear her laughing to herself. They heard more than a laugh. Sarah said, "After I have grown old, and my husband is old, shall I have pleasure?" The Hebrew says "after I am worn out and my husband is old." Then the Lord speaks, which comes via one of the divine messengers, probably the spokesman for the three. The Lord says to Abraham, "Why did Sarah laugh, and say, 'Shall I indeed bear a child, now that I am old?' Is anything too hard for the Lord?" The prophetic word is repeated. By this time Sarah is no longer behind the flaps of the tent. She is outside joining in the conversation. She denies that she laughed; it says "for she was afraid." But the divine messenger says she did laugh.

I want to say more about this great woman of faith, but before doing so there is more to report about Abraham. He, too, is treated in a humorous, if not uncomplimentary way, in the continuation of the passage, which announces the upcoming judgment on Sodom. Abraham begins with exaggerated statements to the divine messenger, who speaks for the Lord, asking: "Will you indeed sweep away the righteous with the wicked?" and "Shall not the Judge of all the earth do what is just?" (Gen 18:23–25). Abraham thinks there are righteous folk in Sodom. Nephew Lot and his family live there. Then begins the famous bargaining, with Abraham asking if the Lord will destroy the city for 50 righteous persons, to which the Lord says "No, he will not." Well, Abraham is not sure, so he lowers the number to 45, then to 40, then to 30, then to 20, then to 10, and still the Lord says: "For the sake of ten I will not destroy it." Abraham ends the bargaining; he does not go down to 5. He could have, because he began with a decrement of 5, but he cannot, for there are six people in Lot's family!

As the story progresses, we find out that no one in Sodom was righteous. Yes, Lot and his two daughters were rescued, but not because they were righteous, but because "God remembered Abraham" (Gen 19:29). So while Abraham can be credited for their rescue, he nevertheless overestimated the righteousness of Sodom and underestimated the righteousness of the Lord. The weighty questions Abraham asked at the beginning about the Judge of the entire earth being just are never answered. So any censure of Sarah's laughter at the messenger's good news must be balanced off with a censure—albeit undeclared—of Abraham's bargain over Sodom.

Returning to Sarah, we must look more closely at her laughter on this momentous occasion. I suggested earlier that the narrator may have intended to depict humor in the incident. There is, after all, humor in the Bible. Edwin Good wrote a fine book on *Irony in the Old Testament*, and Elton Trueblood has written a book on *The Humor of Christ*, which will open one's eyes to humor in the New Testament. Trueblood says most Christians have a misguided piety that accepts wit and humor in the Bible to be mildly blasphemous or sacreligious. Religion, after all, is serious business, therefore incompatible with humorous behavior—to which I would add humorous reporting by biblical writers. The Bible, however, is full of humor, and we need to recognize it.

At the same time, it must be admitted that the best minds have had difficulty in explaining humor. It is a complex phenomenon, as we can see when some people get it and others do not. So while we may not be able to explain it fully, we should nevertheless recognize that it exists. Everone realizes that people do laugh, even if they do not always know why they laugh.

There is an indication in the Genesis story that Sarah's laughter may not have been all that lighthearted. The biblical writer says that "she was afraid" (v 15). Was she just afraid to admit that she laughed? We don't know. I suspect the laugh was a cover for fear and apprehension over a matter that had long caused her pain. All those years Sarah wanted to have a child and was unable to have one; those good years when she could have been a robust mother; those years when other women her age were having children. What is more, she had suffered the abuse of her maid Hagar, who made fun of her when Abraham had children by her. Many years of tension lay behind the present moment.

I remember the first time I realized that laughing could be a release of fear and tension. Linda and I were at Stinson Beach in California with our son David, who was about three. I was walking along with David in shallow water when a big wave came and caught us unaware. Fortunately I had a good hold of David, but the water swept past and I even fell to my knees as the undertoe carried us. I was genuinely afraid. But Linda laughed. I scolded her for doing so, and told her that what had happened was not funny, but dangerous. She then admitted that she could not help laughing, but that she too was frightened.

Laughter is a deep emotional response. Like tears, it can be over joy or pain. Shakespeare knew this; so did Socrates and the Greeks. Laughter is closely connected with terror, says Samuel Coleridge; Kierkegaard, too, noted that the comic and the tragic are very close. It has also been observed that laughter and genuine humor come from an extremely sound mind. Thus I believe Sarah's laughter was a deep outpouring of emotion over what had most tested her in life. Beneath her laughter was genuine fear in the presence of the Lord's messenger. Far from being lighthearted and indifferent, she was deeply involved in a word coming from God.

I believe that by laughing Sarah showed herself to be a healthy woman. How much better to laugh than becoming angry, letting out her pain in bitterness, cynicism, outright disbelief, or defending her many years of hoping without result. Sarah in old age is still on top of her hurt. She is a person of character. More than that, she is a woman of faith, as the preferred reading of Heb 11:11 has it. Her laughter does not disqualify her from being a person of faith any more than Abraham's silence does.

There is yet more to the biblical tradition. There is actually another account in Genesis reporting the news coming that

Abraham and Sarah will have a son. It appears in Gen 17:15–21. Whether this is simply another reporting of the same event, or a different occasion entirely, is unclear. But the thing to note is that here it is Abraham who falls on his face and laughs!

I'm inclined to take the two events as separate, which would mean that Abraham got the news before the divine messengers met him at Mamre. If so, this could explain his silence at Mamre. He had his laugh earlier. At the same time, it often happens that when one person laughs, another is serious. And just the reverse can happen. I noted how my wife and I reacted differently to a dangerous moment on the beach of California. It happens often with husbands and wives when disciplining their children, or responding to a variety of other situations.

The important lesson to be learned from the tradition about Abraham and Sarah is that laughter is not incompatible with faith. Both laughed; both, as the writer of Hebrews says, had faith. AMEN

All Saints

31

"A Bride Adorned for Her Husband"[1]

Text: Revelation 21:2

And I saw the holy city, the new Jerusalem, coming down out of heaven from God, prepared as a bride adorned for her husband

IN THE ANCIENT NEAR East whenever a king died an almost predictible series of events would take place. First, there would be a battle among aspirants for the throne. One would become victorious and be proclaimed king. The new king would then move to consolidate his kingdom, which usually included doing away with enemies. Soon thereafter he would take a wife. He would also embark on a building program, constructing either a new palace, a new temple, or a new city, sometimes all three. The last thing to take place was a giant banquet, at which time new buildings would be dedicated. This would give the king an opportunity to invite people from far and near to see his kingdom. An earlier banquet occurred at the time the king was appointed, but this one was a much grander affair, including visitors from neighboring nations and subjects from distant parts of his kingdom.

---

1. Preached in the Covenant Church of Hilmar, CA, on November 6, 1977.

We know that Babylonian, Assyrian, Canaanite, and Israelite kings came to power through a series of events corresponding by and large to this pattern. 1 Kings 1–8 dscribes how Solomon became king. He and Adonijah were both aspirants for the kingship. Adonijah got his forces together and had himself proclaimed king. At this late moment, Solomon, with help from his mother, was able to get David give him the blessing. Then with his entourage he chose a site and had himself proclaimed king. There was no outbreak of war, but the potential was there. Adonijah and his forces, who were not strong enough, capitulated.

Solomon thus victorious became king (1 Kings 1). He next moved to consolidate his rule, at first giving clemency to Adonijah and also to Joab who supported him. But finally he killed them both. Abiathar the priest, who supported Adonijah, was spared death because he served well under David, and was sent into forced retirement at Anathoth (1 Kings 2).

Solomon then took a wife from the Egyptian Pharaoh, the first of many for this "Don Juan" monarch (1 Kings 3). Solomon then went on to embark on an ambitious building program, which included a new palace and a temple (1 Kings 5–7). The climax was a dedication of the buldings and a banquet lasting seven days (1 Kings 8:65 LXX; Hebrew: 14 days). The biblical account reads:

> Then the king, and all Israel with him, offered sacrifices before the LORD. Solomon offered as peace offerings to the LORD twenty-two thousand oxen and a hundred and twenty thousand sheep. So the king and all the people of Israel dedicated the house of the LORD. The same day the king consecrated the middle of the court that was before the house of the LORD; for there he offered the burnt offering and the cereal offering and the fat pieces of the peace offerings, because the bronze altar that was before the LORD was too small to receive the burnt offering and the cereal offering and the fat pieces of the peace offerings (1 Kgs 8:62–64)

Actually, the pattern is not that unusual to many finding a husband or a wife. You first have a battle of sorts with competing men or women. One emerges victorious, and wins the engagement

"A Bride Adorned for Her Husband"

of his or her lover. The relationship is firmed up: you destroy old pictures of the former boyfriend or give away presents the old girlfriend gave you. Then there is the marriage, followed by a banquet. The building of a house usually comes later, if and when you can afford it.

Here in the Book of Revelation a great cosmic battle for kingship is taking place at the end of the age, and it too pretty much follows the pattern we have described. The battle is between Christ—the Lamb who was slain, but who has now returned in power—and his great adversary, Satan. It takes place on Mount Megiddo (Harmagedon), the scene of earlier battles (Rev 16:16). Christ is victorious, and is proclaimed King of kings and Lord of lords (Rev 17:14).

Christ then moves to consolidate his kingdom, throwing Satan into prison. There he stays for a long time, but gets out to work more havov before being sent to destruction once and for all (Rev 20:7–10). Then comes the great building operation: a new heaven and a new earth (Rev 21:1). This is followed by Christ getting his bride (Rev 21:2–27), after which is a giant banquet (Rev 22:1–2). The river of life and tree of life supply guests with food and drink for all eternity.

The pattern in John's dream is clear enough. But what has always bothered me is the description given of the bride. Throughout the New Testament the bride is understood to be the church, and it is so here. But when John describes her, she is the new Jerusalem with jeweled foundations, jasper walls, and gold streets. Is this really the bride God has prepared for her husband? Sounds more like a wedding gift. Well, it is not that. The bride has been there all the time, but we have overlooked her. She is the many people within the city. The Jerusalem coming down from God is filled with people; it is not an empty structure of precious stones and metals.

The bride is the church. It is the great host who have died in the Lord, who have appeared before the throne of God (Rev 20:11–15), whose names have been found written in the Book of Life, and who are now in the celestial city coming to meet Jesus, the groom. This becomes all the more obvious if we remember that a city spoken of in the Old Testament is never just walls and buildings; it includes people of the city. Even today when we speak of San Francisco we include the people who live there. Thus when the holy city is mentioned as a bride adorned for her husband we must visualize a city full of the redeemed.

What John has done is what so many society writers do when they write a description of the bride for their newspapers. You have all read such articles. They tell you what the bride was wearing, going into great detail about the dress, the cut of it, where the lace was, how long of a train it had, and what sort of bouquet she was carrying. You hear too about how her attendants were dressed. But about the bride herself you hear nothing. Did she have a smile on her face? John has thus told us in great detail what the bride was wearing. His description is all about the jewels and the gold of the dress. And yes, we do hear about the attendants, who are the angels.

Only in 21:4 is there a personal look at the bride. There John describes the expression on the bride's face: "(God) will wipe away every tear from their eyes, and death shall be no more, neither shall there be mourning nor crying nor pain anymore . . ." It is a joyful company coming to meet Jesus and celebrate the banquet.

Today All Saints Day is celebrated in Christian churches across the land. It is a day when those who have died in the Lord are remembered in a special way. These are the ones, together with us, and some not yet born, who will be there when the bride is introduced to the groom and will share in that grand banquet at the end of the age.

As we go to the Lord's table let us remember those who have died in the Lord—beloved mothers and fathers, grandmas and grandpas, aunts and uncles, brothers and sisters, and for some precious children who have gone on ahead. Let us thank God for each of them, for the love they showed when they were with us, for the examples they set, for timely words they spoke. Yes, and let us remember those who spoke the name of Jesus and whose life in countless other ways gave forth the gospel message as they walked

"A Bride Adorned for Her Husband"

among us. And let us remember the brothers and sisters now sitting beside us, some who soon may join the saints in glory, others who will go later.

For those who love and trust the Lord and seek with all their heart to do his bidding in this world, a great and glorious future lies in store. What we do this morning is only a hint of what is to come. Nevertheless, let us partake in this partial feast with joy and anticipation. AMEN

32

Is It Well With Your Soul?[1]

Text: 3 John 2

Beloved, I pray that all may go well with you, and that you may be in good health, just as it is well with your soul

HORATIO SPAFFORD JR. CAME from a distinguished family and was a successful lawyer in Chicago. He was a member of the Fullerton Avenue Presbyterian Church in the city. On November 15, 1873 he put his wife Anna and four daughters, Annie 11, Maggie 9, Bessie 7, and 3 year old Tanetta on the *Ville du Havre*, one of the finest passenger ships afloat at the time, for a trip to Europe. Being busy at work in Chicago, he would rejoin them later.

During the first six days the ship experienced rough seas and dense fog, but on the seventh day passengers awakened to sunshine and calm seas. The following night was calm. Then at about 2 a.m., on November 22, passengers awakened to a loud noise and saw sparks coming from the engine room. The ship had been rammed by a Scottish cargo vessel, the *Loch Earn*. Passengers were in panic, and in just twelve minutes were plunged into frigid waters. Anna Spafford sought valiantly to hang on to Tanetta, and a young male

---

1. Preached in the Covenant Church of Thomaston, CT, on November 7, 1982.

Is It Well With Your Soul?

passenger helped Maggie and Annie as they clung to planks from the wreckage. But all three children were lost. No one knows what happened to Bessie. Anna was one of 28 wearied survivors picked up by the *Loch Earn*. The remaining 226 passengers went to the ocean floor. When Anna Spafford reached Cardiff she wired her husband about the tragedy, saying that she alone had been saved.

In 1876, after husband and wife had been reunited, Horatio penned these words:

> When peace, like a river, attendeth my way
> When sorrows like sea-billows roll
> Whatever my lot, Thou hast taught me to say
> It is well, it is well with my soul
> It is well, it is well
> with my soul, with my soul
> It is well, it is well with my soul[2]

In our text for the morning John the Elder is writing a personal letter to a certain Gaius, a member of one of the churches over which he has jurisdiction. The letter begins with a wish for Gaius' good health, after which Gaius is affirmed with the words, "just as it is well with your soul!" John cannot be sure how Gaius feels at the moment, whether he has some aches and pains, a cold, or a sore foot, but he is confident that all is well with his soul. The following verses tell us why. Gaius is a man who follows the truth and whose life is truth. We read in vv 3–4:

> I was overjoyed when some of the friends arrived
> and testified to your faithfulness to the truth, namely
> how you walk in the truth. I have no greater joy than
> this, to hear that my children are walking in the truth

Missionaries had just visited the church of which Gaius was a member and reported back to John about Gaius. Whereas one church leader, Diotrephes by name, refused hospitality and put pressure on others to do the same, Gaius took them in and treated them well. John is now of the opinion that Diotrephes is hurtful to

---

2. *The Hymnal of the Evangelical Covenant Church of America* (Chicago: Covenant Press, 1950), #365.

the church, not simply because he refused hospitality, but because he was a man of untruth. John says he is spreading false charges against him and others (NRSV). The RSV translates: "he is . . . prating against me with evil words." Prating means "talking nonsense, engaging in senseless and foolish talk, talking excessively and pointlessly."

This is the main issue in the letter. It is not so much about a refusal of hosptality. John had written another letter (2 John) warning a different church *not* to give hospitality to missionaries who deviate from the gospel of Jesus Christ. If they as much as greeted such people they would become partners in their evil work. Gaius is affirmed because he stood up to the prating Diotrephes, and welcomed genuine missionaries of the gospel whom John had sent with an introduction (v 9). Because of this Gaius is seen as a man of truth. The first part of this letter is then an affirmation of Gaius. John knows that it is well with his soul!

At the same time John must issue a warning. Leaders because of their position and influence infect the church if they are bad examples. Even Gaius, who seems to be an exemplary Christian, must be careful. John therefore warns the good man: "Beloved, do not imitate what is evil but imitate what is good" (v 11). He is not speaking an abstraction. Evil refers here to people who are speaking evil words. Gaius is to imitate good people who speak the truth and about whom there is good testimony.

If Diotrephes is a bad example, a good example is found in Demetrius. John says:

> Everyone has testified favorably about Demetrius, and so has the truth itself. We also testify for him, and you know that our testimony is true (v 12)

Perhaps this man is the carrier of the letter. Some have suggested that he was one of the missionaries who had visited. At any rate, he is a person worthy of imitation. The second point of the letter then is this: If one is to stay in the truth, he or she must imitate good and not evil, imitate good people who speak the truth, not evil people who speak untruth.

Is It Well With Your Soul?

How is it with you today? Is it well with your soul? Perhaps you can answer "yes." If not, you might ask yourself whether or not you are a follower of the truth. Pressures to engage in deception today are enormous. There is prating and reckless talk going on all around. Sadly, it can be found even in the church, in which case it is no different from the church to whom John the Elder wrote. Assuming, however, that we are a church made up of people who have wellness in our souls, we must still hear the John's warning. In order to stay in the truth, we need to imitate good and not evil.

Today is All Saints Sunday, a day when we pause to remember God's saints. We need not be reminded that saints are not perfect people. Being "perfect" in the Bible means "being whole, being put together, being complete." Saints are not without flaws, but they are good people, in some cases very good. Horatio Spafford was a saint, for after great loss he was able to pen the words "It is well with my soul."

We do not worship saints as the Medieval Church did. At the same time, there is nothing wrong in seeking to imitate them. In so doing we become ourselves better men and women. We are the poorer if we do not know and lift up people like Augustine, Jerome, Thomas à Kempis, and Saint Francis. Others there are who have lived more recently, and most of us could name a few. We need to remember these people, tell our children about them, allow ourselves and others to be enriched by them.

We are soon to elect church leaders for the coming year. Let us remember how important it is that we have leaders who follow the truth. May we have people like Demetrius and not like Diotrephes, like Phoebe, and not like Sapphira (Acts 5). "The church," as the great Catholic theologian of our day Hans Küng wrote, "is maintained in truth."[3] As for the truth, nothing, no nothing can destroy it. AMEN

---

3. Hans Küng, *The Church Maintained in Truth* (tr. Edward Quinn; New York: Seabury Press, 1980).

Name Index

Ambrose, Saint, 83
Antiochus Epiphanes, 145
Assurbanipal, 4
Augustine, Saint, 128, 171
Behrens, H., 104
Bethge, Ebehard, 137
Blackhawk, Chief, 124
Blatnick, Jeffrey, 148
Bonhoeffer, Dietrich, 8, 136,
    137, 138, 143, 152, 153
Brun, John, 130
Buddha, The, 17, 18, 19
Carlyle, Thomas, 107
Clovis, King, 106
Coleridge, Samuel, 158
Connolly, Miles, 27
Cory, Martha, 68
Daggett, Tim, 149
Daly, Mary, 36
DuBois, Théodore, 79
Eisenhower, Dwight, 45
Esty, Mary, 68
Euripides, 96
Francis, Saint, 171
Fraser, Steve, 149
Frederick III, Emperor, 143
Frost, Robert, 56
Gaines, Rowdy, 148
Gerhardt, Paul, 138
Ghandi, Mahatma, 17
Good, Edwin, 157

Harcourt, Hugh, 68
Hemphill, Gina, 148
Hitler, Adolf, 4, 8, 137
Holmer, Paul, 147
Honan-ja, Rabbi Joshua, 133
Jeremias, Joachim, 80
Jerome, Saint, 171
Johnson, Rafer, 148
Johnson, Rudolph, 148-49
Jones, Jim, 38, 39
Justin Martyr, 28
Kempis, Thomas à, 171
Khawwas, Ibrahim, 50
Kierkegaard, Soren, 158
Koresh, David, 67
Kübler-Ross, Elisabeth, 98
Küng, Hans, 171
Lewis, Carl, 149
Lundbom, David, 111, 158
Lundbom, Linda, 23, 51, 87,
    111, 118, 124, 135, 152,
    153, 158
Luther, Martin, 107, 131, 133,
    139, 142, 143
Moore, John, 38
Nabopolassar, 4
Napoleon Bonaparte, 4
Nelson, P. Raymond, 103
Nilsson, Ola, 123
Noyes, Nicholas, 68
Ohlson, Hulda, 103, 122

Name Index

Ohlson, Otto, 103, 123
Ohlson, Winfred, 110
Palmquist, A. Eldon, 104
Peck, Jennie, 118
Pliny, 129
Pritchard, James B., 12
Rad, Gerhard von, 91
Reagan, Ronald, 7
Ribbing, Lady 122
Rooker, Ben, 118
Rooker, Irene, 118
Sargon II, 12
Shakespeare, William, 158
Shannon, Robert, 148
Sitting Bull, 124
Smith, Huston, 18

Socrates, 158
Spafford, Anna, 168, 169
Spafford, Annie, 168, 169
Spafford, Bessie, 168, 169
Spafford, Horatio Jr., 168, 169
Spafford, Maggie, 168, 169
Spafford, Tanetta, 168
Swedenburg, Romain, 153
Tornquist, Evie, 28
Trueblood, Elton, 157
VanBuren, Paul, 68
Vidmar, Peter, 149
Waldenström, P. P., 77
Washington, George, 7
Zedong, Mao, 8

Scripture Index

OLD TESTAMENT

Genesis
1:2	12
1:3	134
2:9	24
4:4	150–51
5:24	151
6:13–22	151
11	151
12	151
12:1–4	151
17:15–21	159
18	156
18:1–15	156
18:1	18
18:5	48
18:9–15	150
18:15	157
18:23–25	156
18:32	129
19:29	157
22:1	58
40:14	83

Exodus
2:10–15	151
11:7	67
12:22	94
12:50–51	151
16:18	50
30:35	129
32:10	58

Leviticus
2:13	129

Numbers
18:19	129
25:1–15	76

Deuteronomy
5:24–27	19
13:1–5	45
29:23	128
32:6	40
33	110

Joshua
7	76
24	110

Judges
8:22	41
21:25	11, 112

Scripture Index

Ruth
1:16–17	87

1 Samuel
8:1–3	11
8:3	42
11	11

2 Samuel
7	11
18:33	96
20:14–22	75
21:17	134

1 Kings
1–8	164
1	164
2	164
3	164
4:32	12
5–7	164
8:62–64	164
8:65	164
9:26–28	12
10:28–29	12
19:4	96

2 Kings
2:19–22	129
3:27	76
4:1	54
15:32	42

2 Chronicles
13:5	129

Job
6:6	129

Psalms
22	90, 93
22:1	90
22:14–15	93
22:22–24	90
27:1	134
31:5	98
69	9
69:21	93
107:34	128
119:105	134

Proverbs
4:18	135

Isaiah
6:1	42
6:5	42
9:6	28
42:6–7	135
43:1	40
43:3	40
49:6	135
55:6–7	17
60:1–3	135
65:2	18

Jeremiah
1:5	91
7:1–15	141
8:6	60
12:1	46
20:18	96
26:14	142
26:24	142
28	142
34:8–22	55

Ezekiel
16:4	129

Hosea

11:9	37

Micah

6:6–8	77

Malachi

2:10	40

APOCRYPHA

Wisdom

7:3–4	30

2 Maccabees

4	145

NEW TESTAMENT

Matthew

2	28
2:11	29
3:7–8	53
4:1	58
5:13–16	ix
5:13	128–33
5:14–16	134–39
5:16	112, 135
5:23–24	53
6:9	35–40
6:10	41–46
6:11	47–51
6:12	52–56
6:13	57–61
12	13
12:29	13
12:43–45	10–15
12:44	14
13:12	84
13:24–30	5
14:1–2	107
17:5	90
17:20	84
18:23–35	84
21:23	140–44
21:25–26	142
24	61
24:20	61
24:22	61
26:39	48
27:34	92
27:46	89–91
27:48	92
27:51–52	69
27:64–66	105

Mark

1:11	90
3:31–34	86
6:16	107
8:33	43
9:41	94
9:50	133
15:5	74
15:23	92
15:33	69
15:34	89–91
15:39	69

Luke

2	28, 136
2:7	27–31, 28, 29, 86
2:26	86
8:40–42	84
8:49–56	84
9:12–17	84

Scripture Index

Luke (continued)

10:18	59
11:2–4	35
11:4	52, 54
12:15	122–27
12:32–34	127
14:7–11	84
15:11–32	84
16:8	81
16:16	3–6
19:1–10	53
22:11	29
23:34	79–81
23:36	92
23:46	98–99
23:47	81
23:42–43	82–84
24:4	69

John

1:1–15	16–20
1:4–14	134
3:8	37
3:16	77
3:17	58
8:12	134
11:48	74
11:49–50	73–78
11:50	76
18:38	74
19:14	94
19:26–27	85–88
19:28	92–94
19:30	95–97, 104
20:23	56

Acts

5	171
5:38–39	77
13:25	146
20:24	146

Romans

5:8	56
7:14–20	43
8:1–2	7–9
8:15b-16	40
8:22–23	65–69
8:28	45
8:38–39	99
10:21	18
12	136

1 Corinthians

3:1–9	23
3:1–2	120
10:12–13	60
11:23–32	21–24
11:28–30	53
12:4–11	119
12:12–13	119
12:14–31	119
13	120
13:9–10	117
13:11	117–21
15:14	103–8
15:17–18	103–8
15:20	108
15:26	89

2 Corinthians

12:9	50

Galatians

2:2	146
5:7	146

Ephesians

4:13–14	120

Philippians

1:21	109
2:12–13	109–13

2:14–15	145–49	2 John	170
2:15	136		
2:16	149	3 John	
3:13–14	148	2	168–71
4:16	109	2:9	170
		2:11	170
Colossians		2:12	170
4:6	131		
		Revelation	
1 Timothy		6:4	4
4:7	147	7	4
		13	5
2 Timothy		14:6–7	5
2:5	146	14:12–13	5
2:15	104	15	5
4:6–7	97	16:16	165
4:7–8	146	17	4, 5
		17:14	165
Hebrews		20:7–10	165
11:8–10	150–54	20:11–15	165
11:11	155–59	21–22	22
13:14	126	21	13
		21:1	165
James		21:2–27	165
1:2–3	59	21:2	163–67
1:12	59	21:4	166
1:13	58	22:1–2	165
		22:2	24
1 Peter		22:20	19
1:6–7	59		

www.ingramcontent.com/pod-product-compliance
Lightning Source LLC
Chambersburg PA
CBHW050804160426
43192CB00010B/1635